Women's Health and Safety in India

Women's Health and Safety in India

Prof. K. Manimekalai
Dr. A. Ranjith Kumar

KALPAZ

First Published, 2020

Published by

Kalpaz Publications
C-30, Satyawati Nagar,
Delhi – 110052
Ph.: 011-47034999, 9811692060
www.kalpazpublications.com
E-mail: kalpaz@hotmail.com

Printed at: G. Print Process, Delhi

Cataloging in Publication Data—DK
Courtesy: D.K. Agencies (P) Ltd. <docinfo@dkagencies.com>

Women health and safety in India / [editor], Dr A Ranjith Kumar.
pages cm
ISBN 9789353242701

1. Women—Health and hygiene—India. 2. Women's health services—India. 3. Women—Services for—India. I. Ranjith Kumar, A., editor.

LCC RA564.85.W66 2020 | DDC 362.10820954 23

Contents

Introduction

— Prof. K. Manimekalai,
Dr. A. Ranjithkumar—

Health is a primary and more essential input for human resources development of a nation. Gender-specific intervention is essential to address the issues of health which focus on biological differentiation as well as socially constructed norms and beliefs. The health and nutritional status of women in India becoming poorer due to the prevailing culture and traditional practices.

Indian constitution has given equal rights to its all citizens and it recognizes that there would not be discrimination based on the caste, religion, and sex (Article – 15). Still, in reality, it is found that women's status is secondary in society. It gets reflected through various development indicators. Health is one of the important indicators that throw light on society's attitudes towards women. Declining sex ratio is because of, an increasing number of sex-selective abortions, declining nutritional status of women of all age groups, and alarming rates of violence against women are some issues of concern.

Good health is both the means and the end of development. It is identified that improved health contributes to economic growth in four ways. It reduces production losses, permits the use of natural resources, increases the enrollment of children and it frees for alternative uses of e-sources that would otherwise have to be spent on treating illness. This improvement in health is an important factor for nation development. The incidence of inequality in accessing health care services between men and women is a well - known phenomenon around the world. In many countries, women have no or limited access to health care.

When we speak of women's health at global level, we need to use a holistic approach. We know that women are not a homogenous group: they represent different ethnicities, cultures, and socio-economic groups, yet we can find common characteristics among them: exposure to poverty, violence, and chronic illness, they are more likely to die from cancer, alcohol abuse, suicide, cigarette smoking, and obesity. It is very unfortunate that most of the women have little or no health insurance.

It is important that health care professionals and all levels of government be aware of these disparities and find ways of reducing these health inequalities in women, especially those living in remote areas. In the next decades, the international community is set to focus on Universal Health Coverage (UHC) and the Sustainable Development Goals (SDGs) such as goal number 3 "Ensure healthy lives and promote well-being for all at all ages". These goals promote access for all for safe, effective, quality and affordable medicines and vaccines. Both of these major global agendas deal with health, including its economic and social aspects. In building and strengthening health services and systems for women, these issues need to be taken into account with regard to Primary Health Care (PHC). This course focus on challenges in Health Care services, systems and policies that affects women.

The World Economic Forum ranked India as 132nd out of 134 nations in terms of gender equity in health. Furthermore, there remains a disturbingly high Maternal Mortality Ratio (MMR) of 12 maternal deaths per 1,00,000 live births (Ministry of Home Affairs, 2011), despite the country's rapid economic growth rate (Economic Survey of India, 2011). This is an important issue that gender discrimination contributes to poorer health status of girls than for boys is likely to be the main pathway for excess female child mortality. There has been growing international concern on the issue of higher female mortality, declining sex ratio and missing females in India.

Good health is both the means and ends of development. It is identified that improved health contributes to economic growth in four ways. It reduces production losses, permits the use of natural resources, increases the enrolment of children and it frees for alternative uses of resources that would otherwise have to be spent on treating illness. This improvement in health is an important factor for nation development.

The book tackle issues such as scarcity of medical facilities, lack of primary health care, societal and cultural norms, and inadequate policies and funding that often make women reluctant to seek services. Furthermore, we examine the human resources needed in different settings to provide the care and support needed by women. The main objectives of this edited book is to broaden the understanding of the gender gap and inequality in access to health care, services for women, to spread awareness and provide tools and skills for creating better health care services, policies, financing, and management of those services, to view models for accessing health care services for women, and to learn about support programs that provides outreach and education. There are seventeen articles discuss in this book. Each articles concentrate special issues about women's health and women's safety. The following articles discus in this edited book; Menstrual Health and School Absenteeism among Adolescent Girls in Rural India (K. Manimekalai and S. Geetha), & Psychological State of Black Motherhood In Toni Morrison's Beloved (K. Manimekalai, & R.Vanitha), The Malaise of Malnutrition In India – A Meta Analysis Study (P. Sindhuja & K.R. Murugan), An Impact of New Reproductive Technologies In India- A Legal Perspective (S.Shalini), Stress – A Hindrance To Women (R. Radhika Devi & N.Jegatheesan), The Laments Of Kashmiri Pandit Woman's Life (Jiji Paul S), Women's Mental Health And

Stigma (G. Umadevi & Rabina Debbarma), Women's Perspectives on Quality of Maternal Health Care Services: A Study of Government Maternity Hospitals In Hyderabad (Ishratbatool Naik), Management of Menstrual Problems in Siddha System (M. Siva & M. Thiruthani), Factors Influencing In Nutritional Status of Women In India (R. Nageswari), A Study On Attitude Towards Community Service of Women With Visual Impairment Doing Higher Education In Southern States (Kalpana. V), Health Care Access Barriers of Sri Lankan Tamil Camp Living Refugees in Tamil Nadu (Maneesh P & Dr. C. Muniyandi, Health Issues & Problems of Working Women (Ch. Radhika & N. Sai Babu), New Reproductive Technology: Towards A Feminists Perspective (Papari Kalita), Prevalence of Insomnia: A Cross Sectional Study (Mariachristina B &, Anbu N), A Study on Solar Cooker And Its Impact on Women Health in India (D.Swamikannan & N.Periyamayan), and Effectiveness of Structured Teaching Programme on Knowledge Regarding Management of Self Among Primigravida Mothers With Pregnancy Induced Hypertension (Radha .C).

1

Menstrual health and school absenteeism among adolescent girls in Rural India

— ***S. Geetha,***
Prof. K. Manimekalai

Abstract

Menstruation is a vital part of the reproductive health of a woman. There is evident neglect of problems related to menstruation especially in young girls. Lack of awareness and non-availability of adolescent friendly health facilities and other factors hinder the treatment seeking behavior of adolescent girls. Poor management of menstruation affects many girls globally, and especially in low- and middle-income countries. Menstruation was strongly associated with school attendance. Evaluation of a menstrual management intervention that address both psychosocial (e.g. self-confidence, attitudes) and physical (e.g. management of pain, use of adequate menstrual hygiene materials. Challenges associated with effective Menstrual Hygiene Management include lack of access to clean, effective absorbents; inadequate facilities to change, clean and dispose of absorbents; lack of access to soap and water; and lack of privacy. In addition, inadequate social support and presence of taboos can lead to psychosocial consequences of menstruation including shame, fear, anxiety and distraction. These can potentially affect girls' ability to thrive and succeed within the school environment.

Keywords: *Menstrual health, Adolescence, Menstrual knowledge, School girls, School absenteeism, School attendance*

Introduction

Adolescence is a transitional period in every girl's life and it is characterized by rapid physical, mental, and sexual development. Menstruation is a natural phenomenon and is an important indicator of women's health, Menstruation is a normal physiological process that begins during adolescence and many a times associated with various symptoms that occur either before or during the menstrual flow. Many of the adolescent girls experience some problems associated with menstruation, which might indirectly have an impact in their academic excellence, sports activities and their self-esteem. A quality high-school education can transform a girl's future, yet around the world, many adolescent girls miss school or even drop out altogether for one simple reason: menstruation.

Schools often lack the supplies and sanitation facilities, girls need for managing their periods. Girls without adequate health care may feel discomfort or pain. Shame, stigma and misinformation may discourage girls from attending school while menstruating and prevent schools from teaching healthy attitudes about menstruation. Many girls stay at home to avoid being teased. Most schools lack sanitary facilities that are access to clean water points and soap, changing rooms, and disposal facilities. Because of this inconvenience, many girls opt to stay home during their menses, which has negative implications for their overall academic performance and achievement levels. The inability to effectively manage menstruation contributes to absences of up to 4 to 5 school days each month, equating to as much as 20% of the academic year intentionally skipped, simply due to menstruation.

In rural areas, Adolescents do not have access to sanitary products or they know very little about the types and method of using them or are unable to afford such products due to high cost. So, they mostly rely on reusable cloth pads which they wash and use again. Needs and requirements of the adolescent girls and women are ignored despite the fact that there are major developments in the area of water and sanitation. Women manage menstruation differently when they are at home or outside. At homes, they dispose their menstrual products in domestic wastes and in public toilets and they flush them in the toilets without knowing the consequences of choking.

According to the World Health Organization, the availability of adequate clean water and hygiene in schools is essential, for nearly all the Millennium Development Goals, especially in the achievement of universal primary education, reduction of child mortality, and the promotion of gender equality. Poor sanitation at school greatly affects girls, especially menstruating girls, and further creates an unfriendly school environment for them. 355 million is the number of menstruating women in India, accounting for nearly 30 per cent of the country's population. Menstruation continues to be a subject of gender disparity in India. Myths about menstruation are largely prevalent, forcing many girls to drop out of school early or be ostracized for the duration of their menstrual cycle every month. A 2014 report by the NGO Dasra titled *Spot On!* found that nearly 23 million girls drop out of school annually due to lack of proper menstrual hygiene management facilities, which include availability of sanitary napkins and logical awareness of menstruation. The report also came up with some startling numbers. 70 per cent of mothers with menstruating daughters considered menstruation as dirty and 71 per cent adolescent girls remained unaware of menstruation till menarche. A 2014 UNICEF report pointed out that in Tamil Nadu, 79 per cent girls and women were unaware of menstrual hygiene practices. The percentage was 66% in Uttar Pradesh, 56% in Rajasthan and 51% in West Bengal. (Source: *Swachhindia.com)*

"The problems with menstruation in India are that they are similar to a chain of command, related to each other. There is no awareness on menstruation, hence it is considered dirty. Being a 'dirty' occurrence, a menstruating girl is isolated or forced to drop out of school as unlike urban areas, access to sanitary napkins in rural areas is low. This cycle is handed over from mother to daughter but the taboo on menstruation".

Lack of Awareness

Lack of awareness makes for a major problem in India's menstrual hygiene scenario. Indian Council for Medical Research's 2011-12 report stated that only 38 per cent menstruating girls in India spoke to their mothers about menstruation. Many mothers are themselves unaware what menstruation is how it is to be explained to a teenager and what practices should be considered as menstrual hygiene management. Schools are not very helpful either as schools in rural areas refrained from discussing menstrual hygiene. A 2015 survey by the Ministry of Education found that in 63% schools in villages, teachers never discussed menstruation and how to deal with it in a hygienic manner. Adolescent girls across India are remaining unaware of the real reasons for menstruation and the importance of menstrual hygiene. The taboo surrounding menstruation remains a part of their growing up and continues with their daughters. Hence, the lack of awareness is carried forward via generations in India.

Lack of Sanitary Napkins and Adequate Facilities

In a city, availing a sanitary napkin for females aware of menstrual hygiene is a normalized process. Not only are sanitary napkins available in pharmacies and grocery stores in cities, they are commercialized via advertisements so that they are treated as any other product. In rural areas, sanitary napkins are found with difficulty. Most girls rely on home-grown or other readily available material, the latter often being unhygienic and unsanitary. Only 2 to 3 per cent adolescent girls in rural India are estimated to use sanitary napkins. The lack of demand results in storekeepers not stocking up on sanitary pads.

This results in adolescent girls resorting to unhygienic practices during their menstrual cycle, such as filling up old socks with sand and tying them around waists to absorb menstrual blood, or taking up old pieces of cloth and using them to absorb blood. Such methods increase chances of infection and hinder the day-to-day task of adolescent girls on her period.

"It has been seen in rural areas that two-three adolescent girls of the same family use the same cloth during menstruation, after washing and drying it. This is extremely unhealthy and brings numerous health risks. Sanitary napkins are a luxury in rural areas and small towns. Even if available, girls are discouraged from spending on sanitary napkins as old clothes or sand is thought to be good enough for something 'dirty' like menstruation."

Impact on Female Health

Surveys by the Ministry of Health in 2002, 2005, 2008 and 2012 found out that most problems related to menstrual hygiene in India are preventable, but are not due to low awareness and poor menstrual hygiene management. This resulted in development of some serious ailments for adolescent girls. Roughly 120 million menstruating adolescents in India experience menstrual dysfunctions, affecting their normal daily chores. Nearly 60,000 cases of cervical cancer deaths are reported every year from India, two-third of which are due to poor menstrual hygiene. Other health problems associated with menstrual hygiene like anemia, prolonged or short periods, infections of reproductive tracts, as well as psychological problems such as anxiety, embarrassment and shame. Menstruation is such a taboo subject that many women are ashamed even to seek medical advice if they face any health problems due to menstruation. Unhygienic menstrual conditions often result in the development of health problems in girls which are further aggravated due to their inability to seek medical help on time.

Government Schemes on Menstrual Hygiene

From a ban on advertisements on sanitary napkins in 1990, to a full-fledged feature film, PadMan, on a low-cost sanitary napkin entrepreneur in 2018, India has indeed come a long way. It was eight years back in 2010, when the Ministry of Health and Family Welfare launched the Freeday Pad Scheme, a pilot project to provide sanitary napkins at subsidised rates for rural girls. The scheme was launched in 152 districts across 20 states and sanitary napkins were sold to adolescent girls at the rate of *Rs.* 6 per pack of six napkins by Accredited Social Health Activists (ASHAs). The estimated cost for the entire scheme was *Rs.* 70 crore.

A year later, the Union government launched the SABLA scheme across 2015 districts in the country. The scheme aimed at improving health conditions of adolescent girls with menstrual hygiene as an important component. Two years later, under the then ongoing Nirmal Bharat Abhiyan, focus on menstrual hygiene was added as a key component of the sanitation mission. In 2014, the Union government launched the Rashtriya Kishor Swashthya Karyakram, aimed at improving the health and hygiene of an estimated 243 million adolescents. Menstrual hygiene was also included as an integral part of the programme. Under the ongoing Swachh Bharat Abhiyan, menstrual hygiene has been given high importance. The Swachh Bharat (Gramin) guidelines explicitly state that funds allocated for information, education and communication (IEC) maybe spent on bettering awareness on menstrual hygiene in villages. Adequate knowledge of menstrual hygiene and development of local sanitary napkin manufacturing units is encouraged by Swachh Bharat Mission (rural) and self-help groups are help in propagating such efforts. Menstrual hygiene is an integral part of ensuring better sanitation in rural villages. Construction of toilets in households and schools is integral to menstrual hygiene. Under the Swachh Bharat Abhiyan, we are encouraging safe menstrual hygiene practices. Skill development and setting up of sanitary napkin dispensers and incinerators in schools and public toilets are the prime components of the Swachh Bharat Abhiyan, said Arun Baroka, Joint Secretary, Ministry of Drinking Water and Sanitation.

Conclusion

Mothers are the primary source of information, they should be counseled to dispose of their taboos about issues related to menstruation. They should be taught about the ill effects of adhering to taboos related to menstruation. The curriculum on general biology should have more detail on menstruation. Adolescent girls should be offered possible treatment options with adolescent friendly approach. Reproductive health education in the school curriculum should be introduced for improving awareness regarding menstrual care practices. Mentorship program in the school set-up may result in desired improvements providing adolescent friendly health services for sharing their menstrual and other problems. Awareness programs should be conducted by health professionals and teachers through school health programs particularly the rural schools emphasizing the importance of genital hygiene and the remedies for the common menstrual problems which occurs in adolescent age group. Teachers should be trained for the effective implementation of health programs of adolescent health.

References

- Adhikari P, Kadel B, Dhungel SI, MandalA. (2007). Knowledge and practice regarding menstrual hygiene in rural adolescent girls of Nepal. Kathmandu Univ Med J (KUMJ) 5:3826 [PubMed] [Google Scholar]
- Bobhate P. Shrivastava S. (2011). A cross sectional study of knowledge and practices about reproductive health among female adolescents in an urban slum of Mumbai. J Fam Reprod Health. 5:117–24. [Google Scholar]
- Dasgupta A, Sarkar M. (2008). Menstrual hygiene: How hygienic is the adolescent girl? Indian J Community Med. 33:77–80. [PMC free article] [PubMed] [Google Scholar]

- Drakshayani Devi K, Venkata Ramaiah P. *(2017)* A study on menstrual hygiene among rural adolescent girls. Indian J Med Sci. 1994;48:139–43. [PubMed] [Google Scholar]
- *Handra-Mouli and SV Patel. Mapping the knowledge and understanding of menarche, menstrual hygiene and menstrual health among adolescent girls in low- and middle-income countries. Reprod Health. 14: 30 DOI: 10.1186/s12978-017-0293-6. [28249610]*
- Khamdan HY, Aldallal KM, Almoosa EM, Al Omani NJ, Haider AS, Abbas ZI, et al. (2014).The impact of menstrual period on physical condition, academic performance and habits of medical students. J Womens Health Care. 3:185. [Google Scholar]
- Sommer M, Caruso BA, Sahin M, Calderon T, Cavill S, Mahon T, PhillipsHoward PA. (2016). A time for global action: addressing Girls' menstrual hygiene management needs in schools. PLoS Med. 13(2):e1001962.
- Sommer M, Hirsch JS, Nathanson C, Parker RG. (2015). Comfortably, safely, and without shame: defining menstrual hygiene management as a public health issue. Am J Public Health. 105(7):1302–11
- Sommer M, Sahin M. Overcoming the taboo: advancing the global agenda for menstrual hygiene management for schoolgirls. Am J Public Health. 2013;103(9):1556–9.
- 5. McMahon SA, Winch PJ, Caruso BA, Obure AF, Ogutu EA, Ochari IA, et al. (2011). 'The girl with her period is the one to hang her head' reflections on menstrual management among schoolgirls in rural Kenya. BMC Int Health Hum Rights. 11:7. [PMC free article] [PubMed] [Google Scholar
- Mason L, Nyothach E, Alexander K, Odhiambo FO, Eleveld A, Vulule J, Rheingans R, Laserson KF, Mohammed A, Phillips-Howard PA. (2013). 'We keep it secret so no one should know'–a qualitative study to explore young schoolgirls attitudes and experiences with menstruation in rural western Kenya. PLoS One. 8(11):e79132.
- Phillips-Howard PA, Caruso BA, Torondel B, Zulaika G, Sahin M, Sommer M. (2016).Menstrual hygiene management among adolescent schoolgirls in low- and middle-income countries: research priorities. Glob Health Action. 9: 33032.
- Patavegar BN, Kapilashrami MC, Rasheed N, Pathak R. (2014). Menstrual hygiene among adolescent school girls: An in-depth cross-sectional study in an urban community. Int J Health Sci Res. 4:15–21. [Google Scholar]
- McMahon SA, Winch PJ, Caruso BA, Obure AF, Ogutu EA, Ochari IA, Rheingans RD. (2011). 'The girl with her period is the one to hang her head' reflections on menstrual management among schoolgirls in rural Kenya. BMC Int Health Hum Rights. 11:7.

- Sommer M. (2010). Where the education system and women's bodies collide: the social and health impact of girls' experiences of menstruation and schooling in Tanzania. J Adolesc. 33(4): 521–9. 7.
- Sommer M, Hirsch JS, Nathanson C, Parker RG. (2015). Comfortably, safely, and without shame: defining menstrual hygiene management as a public health issue. Am J Public Health. 105(7):1302–11].
- Thakre SB, Thakre SS, Reddy M, Rathi N, Pathak K, Ughade S. (2011). Menstrual hygiene: Knowledge and practice among adolescent school girls of Saoner, Nagpur district. J Clin Diagn Res. 5:1027–33. [Google Scholar]
- Garg R, Goyal S, Gupta S. (2012). India moves towards menstrual hygiene: subsidized sanitary napkins for rural adolescent girls-issues and challenges. Matern Child Health J. 16:767–74. doi: 10.1007/s10995-011-0798-5. [PubMed] [CrossRef] [Google Scholar]
- 19. Health Education to Villages. Toilet facilities in all schools. (2017). Available: http://hetv.org/programmes/toilets-in-all-schools.htm. Accessed: 29 January (2018).
- Government of Tamil Nadu, Department of Social Welfare and NMP. Health Services. (2017). Available: http://icds.tn.nic.in/Convergence.html. Accessed: 29 January (2018).

2

Psychological State of Black Motherhood in Toni Morrison's Beloved

— Prof. K. Manimekalai,
R.Vanitha

Abstract

The novel is a portrait of a black slave woman's experience. The story is important for its demonstration of the concern that slave mothers have for the welfare of their children. Additionally, it is an attempt to understand the forces, both historically and personally, that causes a mother to murder her child rather than allowing her to experience the horrors of slavery. In Toni Morrison's Beloved *readers can see the psychological on the personal and collective trauma of the slavers. The characters though out of slavery, are still haunted by the ghosts of their past, the bodies are emancipated, their minds still carries the burden of memory.*

Keywords: *Post-Traumatic Stress Disorder, Slavery*

Introduction

The presents study aims to depict the sufferings of African–American women. By raising the issue of violence against women in the African-American society, Alice Walker has tried to gain the foreground in American fiction. In her novel, she has projected her women as a victim of violence; however, she brings off a successful change from a fiction to fully responsible protagonist. This study has a function to illuminate the aspects of racial, social and domestic violence against women and to demonstrate how these social paradigms of black existence actually present in the society.

This presence has always been a test case of the nation's claims to freedom, democracy, equality, the inclusiveness of all." African-American literature explores the issues of freedom and equality that are long denied to Blacks in the United States, along with further themes such as African-American culture, racism, religion, slavery, a sense of home, segregation, migration, feminism, and more. African-American literature presents experience from an African-American point of view. In the early Republic, African-American literature represented a way for free blacks to negotiate their identity in an individualized republic.

The search for identity and the clarification of roles veiled by centuries of oppression and exclusion are the themes that are discussed through poignant visual images in *Beloved.* In the novel, this identity is concerned mainly with the question of motherhood. Basing the novel on historical slave narratives as well as on the folk and the classic tradition, Morrison discusses maternal love in bondage, speaking of things that only art can deal with, unspeakable things unspoken to use the title of one of her essays that are brought painfully to the surface. Building her language upon the black oral tradition, Morrison retells the story of slavery in literary terms, a kind of artistic revision of the Afro-American past through the perspective of a black women writer.

Toni Morrison, meanwhile, helped to promote Black literature when she worked as an editor for Random House in the 1960s and '70s.She has also edited books by such authors as Toni Cade Bambara and Gayl Jones. Morrison herself later emerged as one of the most important African-American writers of the 20th century. Her first novel, *The Bluest Eye*, was published in 1970. One of her most famous novels is *Beloved*, which won the Pulitzer Prize for Fiction in 1988. This story describes a slave who achieves freedom but kills her infant daughter to save her from a life of slavery. Another important novel is *Song of Solomon*, a tale about materialism, unrequited love, and brotherhood. Morrison is the first African American to win the Nobel Prize in Literature.

Plight of Black Women in Beloved:

The history of African- America slavery has been presented in an unflinchingly manner by Morrison in her famous novel *Beloved*. In this work Morrison explores the plight of women in male dominated and biased society. *Beloved* documents the lives of African American women who are struggling hard to put their lives back together again, to claim a sense of self that they lost. The struggle of a slave is depicted in visual manner through the point of view of the protagonist Sethe, Paul D, Baby Sugg, who is an ex-slave of sweet home. The author uses historical facts and details concerning the past to make her reader aware of the rich and complex heritage of the African American culture and place of women in it.

She did not let the reader forget the harsh truth about slavery, which includes the master-slave relationship, mother-daughter detachment and identity crisis of slavery throughout the novel. The author combines the psychological and cultural aspects of the black community. And, she explores the issues of identity, and self-possession in a world where slavery has apparently become an unfortunate problem of the past, but emerges, throughout, as a haunting presence. In this novel the writer presents the issue of gender identity and the double oppression, faced by black women and the ways they choose to break free of this oppression, because they are not only women but they are also black.

In the journey of self-discovery, the characters fighting back with this alien world, claiming for a self that is worth respecting instead of existing in the shadows, by submerging their identities. In a slave society the identification of the self is a complicate issue and not possible without communal help. *Beloved* represents the inter-relatedness between the individual identity and the communal identity of the blacks. Sethe is the main protagonist of this novel Beloved. The main theme of this story is about the painful experience of slavery and mental stress, especially about memories of slavery repressed by the ex-slaves. This kind of repression of the past necessarily leads to problems with negotiating individual identity. Sethe Denver and Paul D experience this kind of loss which can be remedied only by recovering the memory of their original identity.

Beloved begins in 1873 in Cincinnati, Ohio, where Sethe, a former slave, has been living with her eighteen-year-old daughter Denver. Sethe's mother-in-law, Baby Suggs, lived with them until her death. Just before Baby Suggs's death, Sethe's two sons, Howard and Buglar, ran away. Sethe believes, they fled because of the malevolent presence of an abusive ghost that has haunted their house at 124 Bluestone Road for years. Denver, however, likes the ghost, which everyone believes to be the spirit of her dead sister.

Sethe spends twenty-eight wonderful days in Cincinnati, where Baby Suggs serves as an unofficial preacher to the black community. On the last day, however, schoolteacher comes for Sethe to take her and her children back to Sweet Home. Rather than surrendering her children to a life of dehumanizing slavery, she flees with them to the woodshed and tries to kill them. Only the third child, her older daughter, dies, her throat having been cut with a handsaw by Sethe. Sethe later arranges for the baby's headstone to be carved with the word ¯Beloved.

Similarly, the period of slavery in the United States was one of the moral reprehensibility, and one that created a similar phenomenon in the slaves. These slaves were subjected to harsh, animalistic treatment, based on pseudo-scientific racial classifications of blacks like ape and primitive. This treatment, coupled with the fear of hopelessness of knowing one could not escape had a massive impact on the psyche, causing a fracturing of the self and even loss of identity. African American black women struggle hard to secure freedom and to understand what such freedom means. The novelist has undertaken a historical and psychological study of black people to establish an independent and free self.

To claim for this free self the black women have to cope with patriarchy, slavery, poverty, racism, social isolation and other forms of oppression. In Toni Morrison's *Beloved*, the return of Sethe's repressed past leads to a complete loss of identity as her fragmented sense of self begins to shatter altogether; however, when she successfully exorcise her past, she finds that without it she cannot have a complete sense of identity. The narrative style in Beloved is the first cue to this fracturing of Sethe's sense of self and the resurfacing of her repressed memories. The novel attempts to seamlessly switch between the past and present in a manner that is disorienting and uncanny. In this way, Sethe's past becomes her present and her present becomes her past. She has no definitive timeline of events, but a shattered temporal sense depicted in an unbroken stream.

Challenges of motherhood and mental stress

Being a mother was a difficult task for of the blacks because they want to prevent their children from the cruel hands of slavery. So that, Sethe attempts to kill herown children. Because, she wants to prevent her children from entering into slavery. Sethe represents the image of such a slave who did not only lost her pride as an individual but also lost apart of her maternity. In spite of the lack of control of black mothers over their children the task of motherhood is still significant. In the patriarchal societies though the role of motherhood is restricted it is still significant. As this novel is focused on motherhood, itshows how the period of motherhood is spent in the curse of slavery. Here, the mother is not able to fulfil her child's first vital need that is the mother can't feed her breast milkto her own child and she can't even take care of her child.

Usually, when babies are born, the mothers take care of her child and try to fulfil her child's need. But, the situation of the black mother is not like that because they can't express their feeling over their children. Being a slave they have to depend on their white master. The slave people live in a place called sweet home. In sweet home all the slaves have lost their identity because of their white master treatment who treat, them as animals. For this they forgot to identify themselves as human beings. The history of slavery left deep pain and scars on the psyche of women when the men were taken away from this cruel situation. As a result of the absence of men, the female characters face pressure that results in mental pain and disgrace.

The task of mothering becomes more difficult for those mothers who are trying to bring up their children with the sense of African culture. They want to raise their children with the identity of their own. And, they want to make their children realize who they are, and who their people are. The role of motherhood in *Beloved* is given more important. Mothers playan active role is remaining the formation of the identity of the whole community. The survival of the Black community depends on the motherhood.

Morrison's novel *Beloved* is lovely based on the story of Mary Garner, a slave who kills her child and attempts to killed herself rather than returning to slavery. Likewise, the protagonist of the novel Sethe kills her child and this murder does not become distant, each time it come closer. In *Beloved*, not only violent acts of white race and Sethe are seen, but also her dead daughter's presence has caused too much given in the novel. At first, the baby girl who has been killed, appears as, ...a ghost in the house, that much we know; it is a ghost that shattered mirrors, that puts its tiny hand prints in the cake... (Bjork, 141). At the beginning of the novel, Baby Suggs states. We lucky this ghost is a baby (Beloved, 6).On the contrary, the ghost's anger comes to their house as a grown-upgirl. She always asks questions about past and wants Sethe to feel the pain in her heart.

Motherhood, childbearing, and child rearing profoundly shaped the lives and experiences of many enslaved women. Becoming a mother was a bittersweet paradox even under optimal circumstances. Motherhood allowed women to experience deep bonds of affection with their children in an institution that all too often robbed them of their humanity. But, on the other hand, enslaved motherhood also contained a slew of painful facets.

Throughout history people have suffered and been through many traumatic incidents. Toni Morrison in the novel *Beloved* has attempted to show us that even after the emancipation the after effects of the tragic events still continues to haunt them. The persistence of the trauma has made them social recluse and they continue to hurt them for the events of the past. Many victims continue to be re-victimised. While some people have adapted them to the new situations of life while some others have held onto the tragic memories, Beloved explores the effects of the traumatic events in life.

Works cited

Primary Sources

Morrison, Toni. Beloved (1999). London: Vintage Books, Print.

Secondary Sources

DeLancey, Dayle B. (1990). "Motherlove is a Killer: 'Sula', 'Beloved', and the Deadly Trinity of Motherlove". SAGE: Scholarly Journal on Black Women 7.2: 15-18.

Bell, Roseann P., Bettye J. Parker and Beverly Guy-Sheftall. (1979). Sturdy Black Bridges-Visions of Black Women in Literature. New York: Anchor/ Doubleday.

Chodorow, Nancy. (1978). The Reproduction of Mothering-Psychoanalysis and the Sociology of Gender. Los Angeles and London: California UP.

Lewis, Desiree. (1992). "Myths of Motherhood and Power: The Construction of Black Women in Literature." English in Africa 19.1: 35-51.

Luckhurst, Roger. (1996). "Impossible Mourning' Toni Morrison's Beloved and Michele Robert's Daughters of the House." Critique 37.4: 243-259.

Lundén, Rolf and Michael Srigley. (1992). Ideas and Identities. Lund: Studentlitteratur.

Page, Phillip. (1995). Dangerous Freedom: Fusion and Fragmentation in Toni Morrison's Novels. Jackson: Mississippi UP.

Peach, Linden. (1995). Modern Novelists- Toni Morrison. London: Macmillan.

Perez-Torres, Rafael. (1993). "Knittmg and Knottmg the Narrative Thread—Beloved as Postmodem Novel" Modem Fiction Studies 39.3&4: 689-707.

Horowitz, M. (1978). Trauma and Recovery. New York: Basic Books, Print.

3

The Malaise of Malnutrition in India – A Meta Analysis Study

— ***P. Sindhuja,***
Prof. K.R. Murugan

Malnutrition

Malnutrition is a complex and multi-dimensional issue. It is primarily caused by several factors, including poverty, inadequate food consumption, inequitable food distribution, improper maternal, infant and child feeding, lack of awareness about the healthy food habits and care practices, inequity and gender imbalances, poor sanitary and environmental conditions, and restricted access to quality health, education and social care services. Malnutrition in India also persists because of the age-old patterns of social and economic exclusion. Besides increasing the risk of infant mortality and stunting in children, malnutrition is also a causative factor for numerous health conditions. The most common deficiency is Anaemia, a condition that can result from a lack of iron intake. It leads to feelings of weakness and fatigue. When combined with other conditions it can potentially result in mortality. In its most severe forms is muscle wasting as a result it reduces the capacity of the individual to work, which disproportionately affects those in poverty and leads to worsening of financial situations. Despite of rapid economic growth, declining levels of poverty, enough food to export, and a multiplicity of government programmes, malnutrition amongst the poorest in India remains high.

Adult malnutrition in India

Particulars	*Underweight <18.5Kg/m²*	*Mormal 18.5-24 Kg/m²*	*Obese >25 Kg/m²*
NNMB (1975 - 1979)	51.8	44.8	3.4
NNMB (1988 - 1990)	49.3	46.6	4.1
NNMB (1994)	47.1	46.3	6.6
NNMB (1993 - 1994)	36.7	51.7	11.6
NFHS 3 (2005 – 2006)			
Women	35.5	51.9	12.6
Men	34.2	56.5	9.3
NFHS 4 (2015 – 2016)			
Women	22.9	56.4	20.7
Men	20.2	61.2	18.6

Source: National Family Health Survey, National Nutrition Monitoring Bureau

Deficiency of Micronutrients in India

With over one sixth of the global population residing in India, one third of about two billion people suffering from vitamin and micronutrient deficiency. Micronutrients are required in small quantities and responsible for vital functions of the human body. India loses around one percent of its GDP due to conditions resulting from micronutrient malnutrition. This situation may become worse in the future — potentially due to an unexpected result of climate change. A study projects that, by 2050 CO2 concentration will reach 550 parts per million (ppm). In those conditions, concentrations of nutrients such as protein, iron and zinc in crops could drop by between three and seventeen percent. This is due to photosynthesis rates being increased, resulting in more rapid plant growth and higher calorie content, at the expense of a lower nutritional density.

Economic Situation and Obesity are Intertwined

Economic growth coincides with decreased rates of stunting and wasting – but also bring with it increased rates of obesity. This is according to a recent study published in *The Lancet Diabetes & Endocrinology* which analyses how the burden of malnutrition changes as countries undergo economic development. In India this situation is complex, as despite the GDP rise of the country in recent years, untold numbers still live in abject poverty. This creates a dual burden of obesity among the wealthier individuals, as well as vast swathes of the population suffering from poverty related malnutrition.

Linkage Between Poverty and Malnutrition

The poorest sections of a society caught in a vicious cycle of poverty and malnutrition which is passed on from generation to generation. Mothers who are hungry, anaemic and malnourished produce children who are stunted, underweight and unlikely to develop to achieve their full human potential. The lack of nutrition in their childhood years can reduce their mental as well as physical development and condemn them to live in the margins of society. These disadvantaged children are likely to do poorly in school and subsequently have low incomes, high fertility, and provide poor care for their children continuing the intergenerational transmission of poverty and malnutrition.

Progress Made in Reducing the Extent of Malnutrition

- The proportion of children with chronic malnutrition decreased from 48% per cent in 2005-06 to 38.4% in 2015-16.
- The percentage of underweight children decreased from 42.5% to 35.7% over the same period.
- Anaemia in young children decreased from 69.5% to 58.5% during this period. But this progress is small.
- Neverthless, many studies over the last five years have exposed the failure of the Indian state to

ensure that its most vulnerable citizens are provided adequate nutrition in their early years.

Existing Scenario

Global Hunger Index Report (2016) and National Family Health Survey

Although great efforts have been made by the Government of India for the past few years to tackle the problem and burden of malnutrition, it is still present in the country and remains a major public health issue. The 2016 Global Hunger Index Report ranked India 97th among 118 countries. As per the NFHS-3 (2005–2006) and NFHS-4 (2015–2016), children aged 6–59 months who are anemic (hemoglobin <11.0 gm/dl) were 69.4% and 58.4%, respectively. According to the **'Food and Nutrition Security Analysis, India, 2019'** report authored by the Government of India and the United Nations World Food Programme stated that despite all the progress made in food security, malnutrition amongst children in India is still remains high.

Child under nutrition in 0-5 years in India

Nutritional Indicator	*NNMB (1975-1979)*	*NFHS-1 (1992-1993)*	*NFHS – 2 (1998-1999)*	*NFHS – 3 (2005-2006)*	*NFHS – 4 (2015-2016)*
Weight for age					
Under weight <-2SD	77.5	51.5	42.7	42.5	29.4
Severely underweight <-3SD	38.0	20.6	17.6	15.8	-
Height for age					
Stunted<-2SD	78.6	52.0	51.0	48.0	38.7
Severely stunted<-3SD	53.3	28.9	27.7	22.0	-
Weight for Height					
Wasted <-2SD	18.1	17.5	19.7	20.0	15.1
Severely wasted <-3SD	2.9	3.2	6.7	6.4	-

Source: National Family Health Survey, National Nutrition Monitoring Bureau. SD- Standard Deviation.

Global Nutrition Report 2017

Global Nutrition Report 2017 reveals that 51 percent of Indian women between the ages of 15 and 49 are considered anaemic. In the same age group 22 percent of women are overweight. The report reveals that 38 percent of children are suffering from stunting and 21 percent are affected by wasting. Stunting permanently reduces a child's capacity for growth. Even more affects brain development which contributes to mental health problems and prevents them in accessing a proper education. Scientists analysed that at least fifty brain chemicals or neurotransmitters are affected by the inadequate intake of food and micronutrients by the child in his or her first 1,000 days. The impact of inadequate nutrition during this golden period is lasting and irreversible, with effects beyond physical health to affect the child's cognitive development.

Food safety and security is not a priority

According to an audit by the Comptroller and Auditor General (CAG) of India, a lack of adequate equipment and mass shortages of staff at the Food Safety Standards Authority of India (FSSAI) have led to lapsed standards and little error in the testing of food quality. These lapses could foster situations during food production and packaging that allow for diseases such as salmonella and E.coli to contaminate products, posing a significant risk to public health. Contaminated food, particularly in a situation where a large portion of the population is undernourished, poses a huge risk to public health. Contaminants within the food can contribute to diarrhoeal diseases, which, in those that are already malnourished, carry a far greater risk of mortality.

Initiatives To Control Malnutrition

National Nutrition Mission

The Government of India launched **National Nutrition Mission** (renamed as Poshan Abhiyaan) in March 2018.

- It aims to reduce under nutrition, anemia (among young children, women and adolescent girls) and low birth weight by 2%, 3% and 2% per annum respectively.
- It also aims to reduce stunting (a measure of malnutrition that is defined as the height that is significantly below the norm for age) by 2% a year, bringing down the proportion of stunted children in the population to 25% by 2022.
- The policy aims to map various schemes that address malnutrition and set up a convergence mechanism, on information and communications technology for real-time monitoring system.
- National Nutrition Mission is backed by a National Nutrition Strategy prepared by the NITI Aayog with the goal of attaining "Kuposhan Mukt Bharat" or malnutrition-free India, by 2022.

Issues in Poshan Abhiyan

- Despite the modest target, it requires doubling the current annual rate of reduction in stunting.
- A year after it was launched, State and Union Territory governments have only used 16% of the funds allocated to them.
- Anganwadis are key agents in distributing the services to mothers and children. But many States, including Bihar and Odisha, which have large vulnerable populations, are struggling to set up functioning anganwadis and in recruiting staff.
- There is limited access to food for the poor and marginalized.
- As Amartya Sen noted, famines are caused not by shortages of food, but by inadequate access to food. And for the poor and marginalised, access to food is impeded by social, administrative and economic barriers.

- The Mission does not have differential approach in which more focus is needed on the areas where malnutrition levels are comparatively high.

International Agencies

- In April 2016, the United Nations General Assembly adopted a resolution proclaiming the UN Decade of Action on Nutrition from 2016 to 2025.
- The Sustainable Development Goal (SD Goal 2: Zero hunger) aims to end all forms of hunger and malnutrition by 2030, making sure all people – especially children – have access to sufficient and nutritious food all year round. This involves promoting sustainable agricultural practices: supporting small scale farmers and allowing equal access to land, technology and markets.

FSSAI programmes to improve dietary health

- FSSAI has responded to the rising tide of Non Communicable Diseases (NCDs) by launching the Eat Right Movement. This has been influenced by the India State-level Disease Burden report, which noted "dietary risks, which include diets low in fruit, vegetables and whole grains, but high in salt and fat, were India's third leading risk factor for health loss in 2016".
- The programme aims to encourage reductions in "western-style" diets and to promote the consumption of fresh fruits and vegetables. Such a change could have a notable positive impact on the rates of NCDs, as it would reduce a major risk factor.

Recommendations

- The government should provide innovative policy and schemes for improving agricultural produce of traditional crops in the country.

- Health Educator should be appointed to all schools, to create awareness about the health and hygiene and to monitor the health status of children.
- Storage capacity should be improved to prevent post-harvest losses.
- It is important to ensure that the poorest are benefited by Targeted Public Distribution System (TPDS).
- Fortification of government-approved commodities within the social safety net programmes can improve nutritional status of the people.
- Child feeding practices should be improved in the country, especially at the critical ages when solid foods are introduced to the diet.
- Fortification, diversification and supplementation may be used as simultaneous strategies to address micro and macronutrient deficiencies.
- All the major welfare programmes, schemes and policies must be probed through gender lens and need to be gender sensitive.

Conclusion

Malnutrition and stunting raise moral and ethical questions about the nature of a state and society where despite rapid economic growth, declining levels of poverty, enough food to export, and a multiplicity of government programmes adopted in combating malnutrition. If India wants to be malnutrition free, it will not be achieved only through government intervention, but through a Cultural Revolution or Jan Andolan like Kuposhan Bharat Choro (Malnutrition Free India). It also requires organizational, financial, and managerial reforms which look the target people through gender lens. Considering the statement "*if one dreams, it is dream, if all start dreaming, it becomes a reality,*" calls for concrete efforts by all stakeholders to make India malnutrition-free.

References

- Global Hunger Index; 2016. Available from: http://www.ifpri.org> topic>global-hunger-inaccess. [Last accessed on 2019 Dec 19].
- International Institute for Population Sciences. National Family Health Survey (NFHS III); 2005-2006.
- International Institute for Population Sciences. India Fact Sheet National Family Health Survey-(NFHS IV); 2015- 2016. p. 1-6.
- Ministry of Women and Child Development, Government of India. Rapid Survey on Children (RSoC) 2013-2014. National Report 2014; 2014. p. 1-403.
- Mishra C P. Malnutrition-free India: Dream or reality. Indian J Public Health 2017;61:155-62. Available from: http://www.ijph.in/text.asp?2017/61/3/155/214814
- https://www.drishtiias.com/daily-updates/daily-news-editorials/malnutrition-in-india [Last accessed on 2019 Dec 19].

4

An Impact of New Reproductive Technologies In India- A Legal Perspective

— ***S. Shalini***

Abstract

This paper is about the impact of new reproductive technologies in India with its legal perspective. Generally the most important phase in a woman's life is her motherhood. She will be treated with utmost care and concern by her family and friends. Not only the people around her would care for her but also general public whom she faces in her daily life will respect and show their concern as a courtesy of humanity. No matter how a woman is during her pregnancy is being respected more and is considered to be sacrosanct. That too in a country like India, mostly women are treated with more respect , particularly pregnant women are given utmost significance in our society. While this remains to be an irrefutable fact, women nowadays are facing more fertility issues and some even become incapable of giving birth to a child due to various reasons which were not a common scenario in the olden days. As the country is developing technologically and is becoming more people friendly, artificial pregnancy are made possible in order to fulfill the hopes of the women who are unable to give birth. This method of artificial pregnancy is a blessing for women who are incapable of getting conceived, but at the same time it is being misused by people in many ways. In this paper the author tries to figure out how the problems are emerging and in what ways it affects the society, like infertility specialist often recommends expensive clinical tests that are unnecessary for the patient but profitable for the clinic, fertility clinics may use the technology to select sex of child (which are prohibited and punishable) etc., and the author also attempts to provide possible suggestions like how to overcome these problems by creating awareness to people, by enlightening them about The Assisted Reproductive Technology (Regulation)Act,2017 Bill and more.

Keywords: *Women – Importance of pregnancy-Artificial pregnancy – Misuse of technology - The Assisted Reproductive Technology (Regulation) Act, 2017 Bill.*

Introduction

> *"The moment a child is born, the mother is also born. She never existed before. The woman existed, but the mother, never. A mother is something absolutely new."* — **Osho**

As per the above-said quotes, it states that when the child is born, the mother is also born from this. It is evidently known that the motherhood for a woman is absolutely a new and significant phase in her life. She is treated with utmost care and concern by her family and friends. Not only the people around her would take care but also the general public whom she faces in her daily life will respect and show their concern as a manner of humanity. No matter how women are, pregnant women are respected more and are considered to be sacrosanct. That too in a country like India, mostly women are treated with more respect especially pregnant women are given utmost importance in our society. Infertility has a cultural and social impact on the life of couples, especially on women. In the majority, women socially excepted to become mothers to ensure the descendance of the family. Therefore, there is a social pressure on women to conceive. If pregnancy is delayed or never occurs, then women are considered as responsible for this failure.

The childless women often excounter scratched experience rather than men, therefore infertility is always considered as a social stigma especially for women. The childlessness of women is considered as a legitimate ground for divorce which is absolutely unjust. There is a set of customs and traditional belief for the relief of childlessness in all countries. When this being a case, reproduction plays a vital role in human's life.

Reproduction is unique in several ways, and it performs a very important role in the process of immortality. Inability to have children, in general, is considered as a personal failure and tragedy around the world. Infertility does not end the life of a person but it incurs wrecking impact on the life of that person for not ful- filling the biological role of parenthood. While this being so, amidst the developments in the country, women who are incapable of giving birth to a child due to various reasons are not being deceived or disrespected as in the olden days, as the country is developing technologically and is becoming more people-friendly, where even artificial pregnancy is being initiated in order to fulfill the hopes of the women who are unable to give birth.

Growth of New Reproductive Technologies

New Reproductive Technologies (NRT) has grown by leaps and bounds in the last few years. It is now being increasingly available to infertile couples in both developed and developing countries. Furthermore, as the economy has expanded, many infertile couples can now afford for the sophisticated NRT treatment. This has led to an enormous increase in the number of NRT clinics providing care to these couples all over the world. India has probably recorded the biggest growth in NRT centers and the number of NRT cycles being performed in our country has steadily risen over the last decade. In a latest survey, based on the number of applications received for National NRT Registry, Indian Council of Medical Research (ICMR) puts the number of such clinics as 125 in the capital city of India. Officials however believe that the actual figures are around 250-300.

I. Artificial insemination

In 1779, the essentiality of spermatozoa for fertilization was demonstrated by an Italian priest and physiologist named Lazzaro Spallanzani who proved that a spermatozoon contained a nucleus and cytoplasm through a laboratory experiment. It was established for the first time that the embryo develops as a result of physical contact between the egg and the sperm. The real beginning of New Reproductive Technologies (NRT) is also known as Assisted Reproductive Technology (ART) started almost a century later when the first report on human AI was published by Guttmacher (1943). Since then, AIs have been reported for many years only in cases of physiological and psychological dysfunction. Around 1909, donor insemination - another aspect of AI gained popularity. While the procedure of AI was gaining popularity throughout the world, in India Sampat Kumaran reported the first AI in Halliker cows at Palace Dairy Farm Mysore in 1939.

II. Concept of Cryopreservation

The continued development in the field of AI provided impetus for improved methods of collection of semen and its preservation. The development in the cryopreservation protocols for future use culminating into the modern techniques of sperm preservation was a natural outcome of the progression of AI. Until mid 1800s, the efforts to actually freeze sperm did not start. He further established that on thawing of frozen sperm samples, the thawed sperm retained their fertilizing potential and induced normal development of the egg which led to the first successful human pregnancy with frozen sperm. As a result of these improvements, the concept of sperm banking came into existence.

III. In vitro fertilization (ivf) revolution

The upsurge from AI to IVF is a massive one, both experimentally and publically. Semen preparation techniques are developing and intrauterine insemination has became popular, being more safe and painless. During 1920-1930s, the role of hormones in reproduction and conception was substantially examined; this led to the use of synthetic hormone substitutes in the 1940s which today form an essential part of all infertility treatments. The history of early attempts of IVF dates back to 1890 when Prof. Walter Heape reported the first case of embryo transplantation in rabbits in Cambridge university. By the end of the 18th century, the concepts of reproduction became clear and fertilization was described as the fusion of nuclei of male sperm and the female egg and embryo thus created *in vitro* laid a significant milestone due to its potential ability to progress to blastocyst stage, getting implanted and be carried out to full-term gestation. Around 80 years, later Robert G. Edwards and Patrick Steptoe performed the successful IVF in human leading to birth of Louise Joy Brown, the first test tube baby on July 25,1978.

IV. In vitro fertilization - the Indian scenario

The history of IVF in India for infertility treatments has come a long way. Just 69 days after the birth of Louise Brown, Dr. Subhas Mukherjee - an Indian scientist from Kolkata announced the birth of Kanupriya alias Durga following an IVF procedure using cryopreserved embryo on October 3, 1978, world's second and India's first test tube baby. Unfortunately, his work was not published due to absence of scientific evidence. The detailed work of Subhash Mukherjee was later submitted in the form of a report to the Government of West Bengal, India. His significant work in IVF was also presented at the Indian Science Congress in 1978 and was also published in 1978. Dr Mukherjee developed a novel and relatively unknown techniques at that time such as use of gonadotropins for ovarian stimulation, cryopreservation techniques, freezing, storing and thawing the embryos.In 1982, the Indian Council of Medical Research (ICMR) a pioneering Indian organization in the field of Biomedical Sciences took initiative realizing the importance of treatment of infertility and initiated a project (led by T.C. Anand Kumar and Indira Hinduja) at its Institute for Research in Reproduction (now ICMR-National Institute for Research in Reproductive

Health) at Mumbai. As a result, India's first fully scientifically documented test tube baby, 'Harsha', was born on August 6, 1986. Due to ever increasing demand for management of infertility in country led to the mushrooming of the IVF clinics in the country. NRT in India is facing major safety concerns and risks that need to be evaluated at a large scale since in the absence of any regulations, the services offered by the NRT clinics are questionable. To regulate these clinics, the ICMR developed the National Guidelines for Accreditation, Supervision and Regulation of Assisted Reproductive Technology Clinics in India in 2005 which were later translated into Assisted Reproductive Technology (Regulation) Bill, 2017and Surrogacy (Regulation) Bill, 2016.

V. Surrogacy

The procedure started long back however; there is still no legal recognition of surrogacy in India. Till date, only gestational surrogacy has been promoted that also in its nascent stage. In addition to it, the laws related to surrogacy are also in the nascent stage. With the recent growth in the count of Intended parents opting for surrogacy in India, the nation has become the much sought after surrogacy destination.

Categories of Reproductive Technologies:

- ***Artificial insemination***

Artificial insemination, also known as intrauterine insemination (IUI), is used to treat women who have normal and healthy fallopian tubes, but for unknown reasons cannot conceive. This may be due to mechanical difficulties with intercourse – for example a man is not able to achieve an erection or has structural problems of the penis after trauma or surgery. Artificial insemination might also be used when semen has been frozen due to a male partner's absence or prior to cancer treatment.

- ***In vitro fertilization (IVF)***

IVF is used in a range of circumstances to assist with conception but is often the only means of achieving pregnancy for women whose fallopian tubes are blocked. In IVF, the woman's eggs are collected, along with sperm from the male partner or donor. The egg and sperm are left in a culture dish in the laboratory to allow the egg to be fertilized. If fertilization occurs and an embryo develops, the embryo is then placed into the woman's uterus in a procedure called an embryo transfer.

- ***Surrogacy***

Surrogacy is a form of ART in which a woman, the surrogate carries a child for another person or couple with the intention of giving the child to that person or couple after birth.

- ***Gamete Intrafallopian Transfer (GIFT)***

GIFT was launched as a more 'natural' version of IVF. Instead of fertilization occurring in a culture dish in a laboratory, the woman's eggs are retrieved from her ovaries and inserted between two layers of sperm in fine tubing. This tubing is then fed into one of the woman's fallopian tubes, where the egg and sperm are left to fertilize naturally. GIFT is no longer commonly used. However, it is sometimes used as an option for couples who don't want to use IVF for religious reasons, providing that the woman's fallopian tubes are functioning.

- ***Intracytoplasmic Sperm Injection (ICSI)***

ICSI is used for the same reasons as IVF, but especially to overcome sperm problems. Essentially, ICSI follows the same process as IVF, except ICSI involves the direct injection of a single sperm into each egg to achieve fertilization.

- ***Pre-Implantation Genetic Testing (PGT)***

Pre-implantation genetic testing (PGT) is a technique used in IVF to help people reduce their risk of passing on a known genetic condition.

There are two types of PGT:

- PGT for monogenic/single gene defects (PGT-M) is used to identify embryos that are not affected by a 'faulty' gene that can lead to disease.
- PGT for chromosomal structural rearrangements (PGT-SR) is used to identify embryos that have the correct amount of genetic material.

PGT-M and PGT-SR are also known as pre-implantation genetic diagnosis (PGD).

In PGT, embryos are generated through the process of IVF or ICSI and then one or two cells are removed from the embryo and are screened for a genetic condition. Embryos unaffected by a particular genetic condition may then be selected for transfer to the woman's uterus.

Legal Validity and Consequence of New Reproductive Techonolgies

The advantage of new reproductive technologies is rampant now a days, on other hands the same is distorted miserably. It is pertinent to note that the commercialization of new reproductive technologies are increasing day by day. Annormously rewarding experience, change into incredible which money can obtain. The best example for the misuse of NRTs is completely for monetary gain and is the thriving of **"Reproductive Supermarket"** in the United States. Moreover the question has been raised on how far the new reproductive technologies are legal in India. Questions have also been raised on the effectiveness, safety, availability and costs of these procedures, as well as many ethical and legal aspects of their use.

While the Delhi High Court ruled down section 377 of the IPC in 2009, granting same sex relationships a legal status, the Supreme Court of India set aside the High Court's ruling in 2013. By limiting surrogacy only to those physically incapable of maintaining a pregnancy, so-called "socially infertile" women are disqualified under the 2016 Bill. In the Puttaswamy judgment the bench reiterated the position adopted by the three-judge bench in the Suchita Srivastava case which upheld that reproductive rights include the woman's right to privacy, dignity and bodily integrity. The Suchita Srivastava case arose in the context of the Medical Termination of Pregnancy Act (1971) (MTP Act) this Act governs abortions in India. The MTP Act permits abortion where the continuance of the pregnancy will cause "grave injury to mental or physical health." In countries where the sociocultural construction of motherhood (and related issues of access and validation) are inextricably linked to the birth of a son, couples may want not just a biological child, but also a child of a particular sex. Further, the concerns posed by these technologies have compounded the accompanying ethical challenges. In addition to the selection of the sex of the child, other traits like eye colour, skin colour, and hair colour can be, and are being, chosen. Thus, the reproduction of 'designer babies' or 'tailor-made babies' has become a distinct possibility. The separation of reproductive body parts – wombs and oocytes (that is, different women acting as genetic and gestational mothers) – also has implications for the global economic market. Through the commodification of women's bodies, it is now possible for a California-based couple of Japanese origin to hire a surrogate in India to have a 'biological child', possibly using donor sperm. A mapping of this reproductive market reveals long international chains of varied actors and agencies, often employing aggressive promotional strategies. 7,000-8,000 surrogacy clinics operate in Delhi. Most of them operate illegally, according to estimates,

- Around 10,000 foreign couples visit India a year to commission surrogacy with nearly 30% being single or homosexual
- Rs 2.5-6 lakh is the amount charged by surrogates in India

- $400mn is the surrogacy industry's value in India as per estimates

No legislation currently regulates NRT in India. In 2002, the Indian Council of Medical Research (**ICMR**) laid out guidelines for surrogacy. Further, in 2005, the ICMR issued the 'National Guidelines for Accreditation, Supervision and Regulation of ART Clinics in India' (**ICMR Guidelines**), which *inter alia*, prescribed the conditions that ART clinics need to comply with. Both the above initiatives did not have any legislative backing. Thereafter, the Assisted Reproductive Technology Bill (**ART Bill**) was first proposed in 2008, with the final version being brought out in 2017. The Surrogacy (Regulation) Bill, 2016 (**Surrogacy Bill**) was passed by the Lok Sabha in December 2018 and is currently pending Rajya Sabha approval.

According to the Assisted Reproductive Technology (Regulation) Bill, 2017, Chapter IV, Para 37, Subpara 7(a), "Assisted Reproductive Technology services shall not be available to a woman below the age of 18 years and above the age of 45 years".

The government has also said that the child born to a foreigner married to an Indian citizen by sperm or egg donation, or surrogacy in India, then the child will not be an Indian citizen, despite being born in India, and will be entitled to Overseas Citizenship of India under Section 7A of the Citizenship Act, 1955.

Suggestions

- Since there is no act to regulate or monitor New reproductive technology, this paper suggests to enact new legislation or approve the existing ART bill which has been pending for Approval for long time.
- The government shall form new vigilance department for this emerging industry to monitor the professionals, private organization and also to ensure negligence-free function in the industry.

- Vigilance department shall be empowered with sufficient power necessary for them to redress the grievances and to necessary action without any delay.
- There shall be regular inspection by proper officer on the activities carried out in the fertility center
- Only specialized medical practitioners shall be entitled to obtain approval from the government to run these centers.
- NRT shall be implemented in government hospitals also so that even poor people can get access to it.
- Minimum percentage of free services shall be rendered to poor by private medical centers.
- Disclaimer or undertakings are the only loophole where the medical neglectors are escaping from the eye of law, hence the act must be passed.
- Government shall make Awareness about NRT in the rural and urban areas.
- Childlessness should not be treated as a deficiency of a couple alone henceforth society shall change their view regarding it.
- Illegal agents and brokers who mislead the surrogate mothers must be penalized with grave punishment.
- Consideration to surrogate mother shall be fixed in a standard ceiling.
- proper screening must be done before treating surrogate mother.
- Patient shall be made aware of all the test to be taken on them before undergoing any such test.
- The use of reproductive technologies and surrogacy arrangements needs to be regulated. The law should promote transparency by incorporating the principle of accountability. Ethical practices should be encouraged. There is definitely a need for regulation.

Conculsion

Since ages infertility has remained a social taboo. The rapid evolution of NRT has became the healing achievement all through the world as a treatment for infertile couple. The social and cultural structures that surround women's lives has been changed in many ways. This paved way to rise a question that it is all because of the development of reproductive technology. Some of these NRTs challenge the even now prevailing as a definition of women as reproducers. The issues surrounding pregnancy, childbirth and motherhood are complicated. The, question to be addressed is that Despite the problems associated with NRTs, why do some women want to use them. Because the matter of pregnancy plays a 'significant role in women's life in our country If she fails in that she will be treated as a sinner in the society. Just because the infertility has been overrated now a days, the NRT has been misused miserably. One of the best example is a 74-year-old woman recently became the oldest-ever to give birth after she delivered twins at a hospital in Andhra Pradesh's Guntur town last week. The woman, who conceived through the In Vitro Fertilization (IVF) process, delivered twin babies at the Ahalya Nursing Home. A team comprising four doctors performed the Caesarean-section operation. There is an urgent need to revisit the Artificial Reproductive Technology (ART) Bill, 2017, which has not received Parliament's approval so far. Thus it is the need of an hour to introduce any guidelines by medical council with this regard or as discussed above, enactment shall be made without any delay to ensure regulation of new reproductive technology.

Reference

- The Assisted Reproductive Technology Bill, 2017(**ART Bill**)
- The Surrogacy (Regulation) Bill, 2016 (**Surrogacy Bill**)
- The Citizenship Act, 1955.
- THE INDIAN PENAL CODE 1908.
- Chandra N. When you cannot produce a baby, design it! Over 500 babies born each month in Delhi fertility clinics. Mail Today. 2013

- Johnston DR. The history of human infertility. *Fertil Steril* 1963; *14* : 261-72.
- Guttmacher AF. The role of artificial insemination in the treatment of human sterility. *Bull N Y Acad Med* 1943; *19* : 573-91.
- Ga-sinovich AE, Glushakova TI. Discovery of the nature of the process of fertilization and of the role of nuclear structures in this process (on the centenary of the discovery). *Tsitologiia* 1976; *18* : 655-67.
- Steptoe PC, Edwards RG. Birth after the reimplantation of a human embryo. *Lancet* 1978; *2* : 366.
- Mukherjee S, Mukherjee S, Bhattacharya SK. The feasibility of long term cryogenic freezing of viable human embryos – A brief pilot study report. *Indian J Cryogenics* 1978; *3* : 80
- Anand Kumar TC, Hinduja I, Joshi S, Kelkar MD, Gaitonde S, Puri CP, *et al. In vitro* fertilization and embryo transfer in India. *ICMR Bull* 1986; *16* : 41-3
- Venkatesan J. Supreme Court sets aside Delhi HC verdict decriminalising gay sex. The Hindu. 2013 Dec 11.
- *Justice K S Puttaswamy v Union of India* WP(C) No.494/2012.
- *Suchita Srivastava &Anr v Chandigarh Administration,* (2009) 11 S.C.C. 409.
- https://www.indiatoday.in/mail-today/story/now-foreigners-cant-hire-wombs-in-india-266222-2015-10-04
- https://corporate.cyrilamarchandblogs.com/2019/04/surrogacy-bill-and-art-bill-boon-or-bane/#more-2751
- http://indiansurrogatemothers.com/history-surrogacy-india/19
- https://www.varta.org.au/information-support/assisted-reproductive-treatment/types-assisted-reproductive-treatment
- https://shodhganga.inflibnet.ac.in/bitstream/10603/15157/6/06_chapter%202.pdf
- https://pdfs.semanticscholar.org/24ef/219c1ab88ec0cb10e71da25a698bf278c7e4.pdf

5

Stress: A Hindrance to Women

— ***Dr. R. Radhika Devi,***
N. Jegatheesan

Introduction

Stress is a normal part of life. In small quantities, stress is good; it can motivate one and help them to become more productive. On the other hand, too much stress, or a strong response to stress can be harmful. How one can perceive a stress provoking event and how one react to it determines its impact on their health. One may be motivated and invigorated by the events in their lives, or one may see some as "Stressful" and respond in a manner that may have a negative effect on their physical, mental, and social well-being.

Stress is defined as 'the pattern of emotional states and physiological reaction occurring in response to demand from within or outside on organization'. The stressor, on the other hand, is considered to be 'a condition or situation that elicits a negative response such as anger, frustration, anxiety or tension'. The stress in the work place is quite common and can be measured through different sources. Nature of work, time pressure, role ambiguity, role conflict, career progress and communication are considered as major sources of pressure in the life of an Information System professional. Anxiety ultimately causes stress that leads to different types of strain and finally hampers the performance of the employees. Stress, not only affects the efficiency of the employees, but also causes ailment and other physical or emotional problems as well.

Stress can be defined as:

"*The way your body responds to the demands of your life style' i.e., the effect of wear and tear on your body.*" The majority of people think of stress as a mental state but it is in fact, very largely, a physical condition. When a person is subjected to a stress producing effect known as stressor (a challenge, pressure, stimulus, external influence, and the like.) it is registered in the brain. The brain gives various parts of the body instructions for a chain of reactions known as stress reaction or stress response.

Objectives

The main objectives of the study were

- To find out the stress level of employed and unemployed women.
- To measure perception level of respondents towards the stress level.

Hypothesis

For the present study following hypothesis were formulated.

H0: There is no significant difference in the perception of the different groups of members classified according to agc, cducation, income, family size and martial status regarding Stress level

Sample Size

The sample size consisted of 100 women in which 50 were employed and 50 House wives (unemployed). The method adopted is convenient sampling method.

Sources of Stress

One can experience stress from four basic sources:

- **The Environment** – The environment can bombard one with intense and competing demands to adjust. Some of the sources of environmental stressors are weather, noise, crowding, pollution, traffic, unsafe and substandard housing and crime.
- **Social Stressors** – one can experience multiple stressors arising from the demands of the different social roles they occupy, such as parent, spouse, caregiver and employee. The major sources of social stressors are deadlines, financial problems, job interviews, presentations, disagreements, demands for your time and attention, loss of a loved one, divorce and co-parenting.
- **Physiological** – situations and circumstances affecting one's body can be experienced as physiological stressors. Physiological stressors sources include rapid growth of adolescence, menopause, illness, aging, giving birth, accidents, lack of exercise, poor nutrition and sleep disturbances.
- **Thoughts** – a person brain interprets and perceives situations as stressful, difficult, painful or pleasant. Some situations in life are stress provoking, but it is our thoughts that determine whether they are a problem for them or not.

Effect of Stress

Stress response

The stress reaction can be described as a sequence of response of changes within the body:

- Shallower, quick breathing
- Faster heart beat
- Rise in blood pressure

- Reduction in the blood supply to hands and feet
- Increase in body metabolism
- Faster clotting of blood
- Increased blood flow to the muscles
- Reduction of blood supply to stomach and abdomen
- Tensing of muscle
- Sharpening of all senses
- Reduction of tension in bowels and stomach function
- Reduction in the efficiency of the immune system

All these changes in the body have a marked effect on the brain and this can cause an alert mental state, leading to:

- Faster activity of brain
- Improvement of short term judgment
- Faster decision making
- Improved memory powers
- Sharper focusing of the attention

Women and Stress

There are many causes of stress both men and women carve up such as finance matters, work security, health, and relationship issues. Perhaps a little more unique to women are the many roles they take on. In today's society, women's roles often include family obligations, care giving for children and/or elderly parent and work responsibilities as well as other roles. As demands increase to fulfill these roles, women feel overwhelmed with time pressures and unmet obligations. They may feel a sense of failure in not being able to meet expectations for themselves and others. Oftentimes women spend more time meeting the needs of others rather than nurturing their own needs. If functioning at high stress levels, women may not even recognize what their needs are.

The latest study done by Nielsen reveals that Indian women are the most stressed in the world today. An overwhelming 87% of Indian women said they felt stressed most of the time, and 82% had no time to relax.

In addition to the health symptoms that are brought on by stress, these additional health problems can develop in women exposed to stress over long periods of time.

- **Depression and Anxiety:** Women have higher rates of these conditions and other psychological disorders including panic disorder and obsessive compulsive disorder than men.
- **Heart Problem:** Stress increases blood pressure and heart rate.
- **Headaches and Migraine:** Tension headaches are more common in women than men.
- **Obesity:** Women are more prone to stress-related weight gain than men.
- **Bowel Problems:.** Stress can lead to such bowel problems as irritable bowel syndrome.
- **Pregnancy Issues.** Women with higher stress levels have a more difficult time becoming pregnant than women with lower stress levels.
- **Menstrual Problems.** Premenstrual syndrome is more severe with increasing stress levels.

Women Stressed than Men

Women are twice more likely to experience major depression than men. They also suffer three times more from anxiety disorders and they even attempt suicide. The reasons for these gender differences are not clear, and some believe such statistics are exaggerated because females are more "sensitive" and therefore more likely to report such symptoms. On the other hand, a variety of observations tend to confirm that these disparities are valid, such as the following half dozen.

1. Hormonal differences are usually cited as the major explanation. Compared to men, women experience much more fluctuation in hormone levels that are associated with symptoms of depression. In addition to premenstrual disorder, up to 15% experience postpartum depression. Depression is so common during the menopause, that involutional melancholia was an established psychiatric diagnosis up until 1980. Women are also more apt to suffer from hypothyroidism, which is often associated with depression.

2. Women have a stronger genetic predisposition for depression than men based on identical and fraternal twin studies, as well as documented and detailed family history records.

3. Women tend to be more involved in personal relationships than men and suffer more when they are disrupted. More married women and housewives have increasingly entered the workforce and find it difficult to juggle job and family responsibilities, such as caring for an elderly relative. A major European study covering over 30 countries with a combined population of 514 million people recently reported that depression in middle-aged women had doubled in 40 years because of these pressures. Women between the ages of 25 and 40 were three to four times more likely to become depressed than men.

4. Women live longer than men and extreme old age is often associated with bereavement, loneliness, poor physical health, and other factors that predispose to depression.

5. Women are more likely than men to consult a physician if they do not feel well or have symptoms of depression, and are therefore more likely to be diagnosed. There is also some evidence that both male as well as female physicians are more apt to make a diagnosis of depression in women than men with identical complaints.

Findings

Age and Stress Level Perception Score

To test the null hypothesis that there is no significant difference in the perception of the different groups of members classified according to age regarding Stress level, the Kruskal Wallis Test has been applied. The result of the test is depicted in Table 5.1.

Table 5.1: Relationship between Age and Perception Level

Sl. No	*Stress type*	*Critical Value*	*Significant Level*	*Result*
1.	Work stress	27.745	0.000	Significant
2.	Financial stress	2.661	0.264	Not Significant
3.	Physical stress	0.158	0.924	Significant
4.	Family stress	38.609	0.000	Significant
5.	Psychological stress	26.745	0.000	Significant
6.	Over all	0.985	0.611	Not significant

Source: Primary data.

It could be observed from Table 5.1 that there is a significant difference in the perception of the sample respondents in respect of the Work Environment, Interpersonal relationship, Work stress, Physical stress, family stress, Psychological stress and Organizational stress whereas the Financial stress and Over all stress level has no significant relationship between the age of the respondents.

Marital Status and Stress Level Perception Score

To test the null hypothesis that there is no significant difference in the perception of the different groups of members classified according to marital status regarding Stress level, the Kruskal Wallis Test has been applied. The result of the test is depicted in Table 5.2.

Table 5.2: Relationship Between Marital Status and Perception Level

Sl. No	*Stress type*	*Critical Value*	*Significant Level*	*Result*
1.	Work stress	0.077	0.782	Not Significant
2.	Financial stress	0.169	0.681	Not Significant
3.	Physical stress	0.200	0.654	Significant
4.	Family stress	1.923	0.166	Not Significant
5.	Psychological stress	2.778	0.000	Significant
6.	Over all	1.627	0.202	Not Significant

Source: Primary data

It could be observed from Table 5.2 that there is a significant difference in the perception of the sample respondents in respect of the Interpersonal relationship, Physical stress, Organizational stress and Psychological stress whereas Work Environment, Work stress, Financial stress, Family stress and Over all stress level has no significant relationship between the marital status of the respondents.

Educational Level and Stress Level Perception Score

To test the null hypothesis that there is no significant difference in the perception of the different groups of members classified according to educational level regarding Stress level, the Kruskal Wallis Test has been applied. The result of the test is depicted in Table 5.3.

Table 5.3: Relationship Between Educational Level and Perception Level

Sl. No	*Stress type*	*Critical Value*	*Significant Level*	*Result*
1.	Work stress	8.986	0.000	Significant
2.	Financial stress	3.114	0.000	Significant
3.	Physical stress	7.556	0.000	Significant
4.	Family stress	8.059	0.000	Significant
5.	Psychological stress	1.343	0.719	Not Significant
6.	Over all	3.794	0.000	Significant

Source: Primary data

It could be observed from Table 5.3 that there is a significant difference in the perception of the sample respondents in respect of the Work Environment, Interpersonal relationship, Work stress, Financial stress, Physical stress, Family stress, Organizational stress and Over all stress level whereas Psychological stress has no significant relationship between the educational level of the respondents.

Family Size and Stress Level Perception Score

To test the null hypothesis that there is no significant difference in the perception of the different groups of members classified according to family size regarding Stress level, the Kruskal Wallis Test has been applied. The result of the test is depicted in Table 5.4.

Table 5.4: Relationship Between Family Size and Perception Level

Sl. No	*Stress type*	*Critical Value*	*Significant Level*	*Result*
1.	Work stress	0.533	0.465	Not Significant
2.	Financial stress	1.058	0.304	Not Significant
3.	Physical stress	3.261	0.000	Significant
4.	Family stress	1.937	0.164	Not Significant
5.	Psychological stress	3.831	0.000	Significant
6.	Over all	5.023	0.025	Significant

Source: Primary data

It could be observed from Table 5.4 that there is a significant difference in the perception of the sample respondents in respect of the Physical stress, Psychological stress, Organizational stress and Over all stress whereas Work Environment, Interpersonal relationship, Work stress, Financial stress and Family stress has no significant relationship between the family size of the respondents.

Income Level and Stress Level Perception Score

To test the null hypothesis that there is no significant difference in the perception of the different groups of members classified according to income level regarding Stress level, the Kruskal Wallis Test has been applied. The result of the test is depicted in Table 5.5.

Table 5.5: Relationship Between Income Level and Perception Level

Sl. No	*Stress type*	*Critical Value*	*Significant Level*	*Result*
1.	Work stress	4.430	0.000	Significant
2.	Financial stress	7.973	0.047	Significant
3.	Physical stress	5.682	0.128	Not Significant
4.	Family stress	2.705	0.000	Significant
5.	Psychological stress	2.177	0.000	Significant
6.	Over all	3.875	0.275	Not Significant

Source: Primary data

It could be observed from Table 5.5 that there is a significant difference in the perception of the sample respondents in respect of the Work Environment, Interpersonal relationship, Work stress, Financial stress, Family stress and Psychological stress whereas Physical stress, Organizational stress and Over all stress has no significant relationship between the income level of the respondents.

Coping Stress

Everybody in the world have to suffer with stress at some situation in their lives. One can take various steps to copc the stress in a positive way.

- **Take deep breaths;** This forces you to breathe slower and helps your muscles relax. The additional oxygen passes a message to your brain to calm down and relax the body.
- **Stretch;** This activity can also help to relax ones muscles and make them feel less tense.

- **Write out your thought; Just write** a thoughts or simply writing down the things you are thankful which can easily help you to handle stress.
- **Take time for yourself;** It could be listening to music, reading a good book, or going to a movie.
- **Meditate; Many** researches have proven that meditation which reduces the stress, a time to focus the mind on a positive or neutral thought, can help lower stress. Meditation in general protecting everyone, and free meditation guides are widely available online.
- **Get enough sleep;** The majority of adults require seven to nine hours of sleep a night to feel rested.
- **Eat right;** Eat foods which contain vitamins, such as bananas, fish, avocados, chicken, and dark green, leafy vegetables. Studies show that vitamins can help relieve stress by regulating nerves and brain cells.
- **Physical Activities;** Games and Exercise can relax your muscles and improve your mood. These activities in turn help relieve symptoms of depression and anxiety.
- **Chat with friends or family members;** Friends might help you to find solution to your problems in another ways. One can also talk to the family member about their source of stress which in turn help you to feel better.
- **Get organized;** If the work is disorganized it becomes as a sign of stress, which can also cause stress. Organize both your work and home life and set priority.

Conclusion

People react to stress in different ways. Some are coping much better than others and suffering fewer of the harmful effects of stress. Just as stress differs as a function of the individual, it also differs as a function of one's type of occupation. Some occupations are, of course, inherently more stressful than others. All of the stress-strain-health relationships have an obvious impact on the organization and industry. Occupational stress is becoming increasingly globalized and affects all countries, all professions and all categories of workers, as well as families and society in general. Beehr and Newman define occupational stress as "A condition arising from the interaction of people and their jobs and characterized by changes within people that force them to deviate from their normal functioning." Job stress can be defined as the harmful physical and emotional responses that occur when the requirements of the job do not match the capabilities, resources, or needs of the worker. Job stress can lead to poor health and even injury. When the demands and pressures placed on individual workers do not match the resources which are available, either from the organization or within the individual, stress can occur and endanger that person's health and well-being."

Reference

- Brewer and Landers (2003) : "Relationship between Job stress and Job Satisfaction among Industrial and Technical Teacher Educators": Journal of Career and Technical Education; Volume 20, Number 1.
- Coetzer, and W.J. (2006); Rothmann, S: "Occupational stress of employees in an insurance company": S.Afr. J.Bus. Manage. 2006, 37(3)
- Muntazir M, Neharshi S, Manju P (2014) A comparative study of mental health among working women and house wives. Indian Journal of Health and Wellbeing 5: 1398-1400.
- Hamilton S, Fagot BI (1988) Chronic stress and coping styles: A comparison of male and female undergraduates. J Pers Soc Psychol 55: 819-823.
- American Psychological Association (2008) Stress in America. American Psychological Association, USA.5. Swanson NG (2000) Working Women and Stress. Journal of the American Women's Medical Association 55: 76-79.
- Nevin S, Fatima A (2007) A study into the effects of stress on women's health. Humanities & Social science Journal 2: 104-109.
- Hashami HA, Khurshid M, Hassan I (2007) Marital Adjustment, Stress and Depression among Working and non-working Married Women. Journal of Medical Science 2: 19-26.

6

The Laments of Kashmiri Pandit Woman's Life

— Dr Jiji Paul S

Abstract

Origin of Kashmiri Pandit community covers more than a period of five thousand years. Kashmiri Pandits are Saraswat Brahmins. According to Kalahana, his Rajatarangini explained the origin of the community their beliefs, customs, traditions, socio-economic situations along with certain festivals of Pandits. Before Independence, Kashmiri Pandits lived a peaceful life in the valley and enjoyed all rights available to the citizens. During the communal flare-ups of the partition, their land lordship over agricultural land got eschewed under the tenancy and land reforms initiated by the people's government in 1952 affected a large number of Pandit families. During the year Pakistan sent guerrillas to Kashmir in 1965 under "operation Gibraltar" which lead to a full-scale war. Six years later another war between India and Pakistan resulted in the bifurcation of Pakistan and formation of Bangladesh and subsequent signing of Shimla Agreement under which both countries were to resolve the issue bilaterally. The minority Pandits of the valley became the victims of this operation and they were gunned down indiscriminately, hanged or murdered by other brutal means. Torture, molestation and rape, threatening letters and telephone calls, posters and bit notices pasted on doors and warnings through newspapers for the whole community to leave the valley within short and specified time. Pakistan's sponsored militancy badly affected Kashmiri Pandit women's life. Family relations seem to broken, Divorce rates increased, mentally and physically they become weak, Important thing is, more than 60% woman had lost their peace. They become the victims of stress and manifestation of diseases. Nearly

Thousand female members of this community have been done to death, and nearly three hundred thousand forced into exile. Militancy had taken more than 500000 innocent woman, men and children lives. Every year Central & State Governments spend cores for creating everlasting peace in Jammu & Kashmir. Authorities must implement urgent steps to solve their Mental and physical problems; otherwise in future this may create another challenge against our glorious democracy. In 1991, Pak Sponsored Militancy destroyed the dreams and hope of Kashmiri Pandit Women's life; also it shaded their everlasting peace and security of these Communities.

Key Words: *Kashmiri Pandits, Militancy, Pandit women, Environmental Disease, Exile.*

Introduction

Kashmiri Pandits are a unique set of people and are handsome, civilized, educated, gentle, with good communicative skill. They are intelligent, and excel in whatever they do; they have a role and a mission given by God. They are like the salt of the earth. They have adopted, Saptarishi Calendar (current year-5078), and follow rituals formulated by Rishi Logaksha, as against those of Rishi Katyayan followed in other parts of the country (Pandit R.S, 1963: 71). Kashmiri Pandits were divided into the astrologer clay (Jotish), the Priest (Guru), and those who follow secular occupations (Karkun). The vast majority of Kashmiri Pandits, who belong to the Karkun category, were salaried state employees in the lower ranges of the administration, while others practice agriculture and related occupations (Kaul R U, 1999: 48).

Their thirst for knowledge is an abiding virtue which illuminate many minds and societies. In fact, in the 21st century, Saraswati has become Mahalakshmi. Culture and society of these Pandits can further be structured on the values held by the prominent Kashmiri Pandit Jawaharlal Nehru (Bhatt S, 1995: 68). This community believe and workshop Shiva and Shakti workship and follows Kashmir Shaiva Darshan for spiritual purposes and the Vedas for rituals. Apart from the common festivals and religious functions like Diwali, Dussehra, Ganesh and Lakshmi

Pooja, they have some peculiar festivals. The most important of this is Shiva Ratri, a socio-religious function celebrated over a period of a fortnight (the dark fortnight of Falguna of the lunar calendar). The New Year's Day is celebrated on the first day of the Bright fortnight of Chaitra (Ahamed Feroz, 1998 79-80).

Odyssey of Kashmiri Pandits

Kashmiri Pandits at no stage of history ceased to make contributions. The gifts supplied to northern India by Haimastavas of Sabhaparvas of Mahabarata included even Kashmiris. They presented silks and woolens. Kashmiri Pandit monks and missionaries dared the trek across and spread the message of the great Buddha at the cost of their lives. A few of the notables were Gautam Sangha, Buddhayasas, Vimalaksha Buddajiva, Shakyashri Badhra, Ratanvira and ShamaBhatta etc. Even Kumarijiva, referred to in China as "one of the four suns of Buddhism" received education in Buddhist thought and tradition at the hands of Kashmiri scholars (Kapur M L, 1983: 46).

It was he who, along with a group of Kashmiri Pandit Scholars made Kucha a seat of Buddhist learning in Central Asia. Kashmir once represented a laboratory in which Buddhist thought and philosophy were dissected at the hands of learned Kashmiri Pandit scholars. It attracted chain of scholar-pilgrims from distant lands (Bhattachajea Ajith, 1994 : 113). HuenTsiang, Che-mong, Fa-yong, and Qu-kong all visited Kashmir to study Sanskrit and Buddhist philosophy. Kanishka chose it as the proud place for a Buddhist conference. The philosophical thought which Kashmiri Pandit scholars propounded and advocated was ever-evolving and growing. At the end of Eighth Century, Buddhism in Kashmir lost its glory and the new thought of "Advaita" of Sankaracharya made an impact, Kashmiri scholars gave monastic interpretation to Saivism in Kashmir (Pream Shankar Jha, 1997: 49). Kashmir Shaivism is possibly the most rational, logical and pragmatic science of spirituality propagated anywhere in the world. Instead of saying that the world is illusory, it declares emphatically that the world is as real as God. Kashmiri Pandits culture includes festivals, language, cuisine, rituals, music, literature and customs. They preserve distinct cultural identity, document it, and practice it, pass it on to their children, and are proud of it. They patronize artists and writers, buy their books and tapes, go and watch them or listen to them and encourage them with acclaim and recognition (Pant kusum, 2009: 107-108).

Pandits become victims of Militancy

Militancy destroyed, the lives of Kashmiri Pandits. After the independence, Pakistan send tribal peoples to grab Kashmir with the help of its army. It created so much conflicts and disputes between both nations. In 1989 militancy conducted massive attacks against minority Pandits. Fundamentalist stole their land and homes, even their right to live also. The five thousand old Saraswth Brahmin communities had lost their traditions, customs and civilizations. Pandit communities are in exile. They are getting some subsidies and financial helps from authorities. But they had lost their freedom. Militancy had badly affected the life of pandit women's. They are living in two room tin shaded camps. Physically and mentally they are week. Their children have become the victims of great fear. Family envisages are broken, not getting proper education, all basic facilities are denied due to militancy. Pandit women had lost their valuable dreams and hopes about family (Nelson Thomas: 2000: 148).

Pandit women in Exile

The Kashmiri Pandit Women, who have entered the twenty fourth year in exile, appeal to the conscience of the civilized world to grasp the grim tragedy that has kept the Kashmiri Pandit women in exile. The worst victims were the women. The grave human tragedy began with religious persecution and genocide, kidnappings and a spare of killings, torture, rape, murder and molestation of women, even little children and young girls were not spared. The communal carnage, the forced exodus, the changed milieu, alien and hostile environment, along with a torn social fabric, poor shelter, lack of privacy and security have resulted in serious health traumas. One hundred per cent of the exiled Kashmiri Pandit Women are affected with health syndromes. The old and the infirm have met a premature death, dying for want of health and family support. A large number have suffered mental breakdown due to the stress, terror, violence and genocide (Data collected from J&K State Department).

The genocide has badly affected Pandit women. Many women become the victim of panic problems like mental and physical disorders, depression problems and anxiety disorders. It is observed that many women are using toxic medicines for deep sleep in order to save them from sleepless nights (Data collected from J&K State Department).

The most alarming phenomenon has been a very high occurrence of ovarian failure and premature menopause leading to greatly reduced fertility span, resulting in a negative growth. This has been further accentuated by a high death rate, unnatural deaths, premature aging, low birth rate due to contraception, elective abortion, late marriages, sexual deprivation due to stress and lack of privacy, reduced desire and therefore reduced conception. 400 consecutive females with menopausal symptoms in exile were compared with equal number who developed menopause before exile. More than a third (36%) of females is infertile by the time they reach 40 years' age in exile.

High divorce rate in exile

Marriages are arranged by families. Sub caste endogamy is a prescription, and within the sub caste the rule of gotra exogamy is normally observed. The preferred type of marriage is between completely unrelated families. Bride givers accept a deferential role for themselves and offer dowry to bride takers. Owing to the shortage of women, however, Marriages by exchange between bride givers and takers, though not well thought of, are about as frequent as the favoured type of marriage. Very rarely a man may buy himself a wife, but such an arrangement is never publicly acknowledged (Amy Waldan, 2002: 167).

Traditionally widows did not remarry but in the last couple of generations some cases of widow remarriage have occurred, involving particularly young childless widows. Girls leave their parental home on marriage and go to live with the husband and his parents. If the husband is employed away from home, the bride begins her life as a married woman by living with her parents-in-law for about a year before joining her husband, who may however visit her at home. Occasionally, when a couple has no sons, they may arrange for their daughter (or one of their daughters, if there are several) to marry patriuxoriocally. Her husband then comes to live with his parents-in-law and looks after them. Since Pandits consider marriage a sacrament, the notion of divorce is absent.

The matrimonial court records also show the unprecedented trend in marriage disputes among Kashmiri Pandit community. Out of over 1200 cases registered by court, 430 have been initiated by Kashmiri Pandits in the year 2007. Maximum number of couples that approached the court for divorce is in the age group of 24-40 years. It is the children in the family who have to suffer. Children become the scapegoat due to the dispute between parents. They are dragged to court for no fault of theirs. Their future has been put at stake (Tikko Ramesh, 2006: 183).

Environmental Disorders

Environmental problems badly affected the pandit women. Heat-related syndrome like strokes, Heat exhaustion,

Cramps, Dehydration, Solar exposures, Sunburns, solar dermatitis, Solar pigmentation, Predator attacks, snake bites, scorpion bites. Air borne diseases of Allergic syndromes new antigens in the environment pollen, parthenium or congress agars etc. Respiratory infections like tuberculosis, bronchitis, and pneumonia, Skin infestations Scabies, fungi, yeast, boils abscesses, Water borne diseases(water supply of the camps contaminated with effluent and waste), Hepatitis, diarrhoea, dysentery, amoebiasis, giardiasis, typhoid etc.

All these factors leads to the release of hormones and chemicals in the body with deleterious consequences on the organ systems giving rise to numerous stress syndromes, both mental and physical. The visit of all Pandit camps in J&K states revealed that still they are living fearful conditions. Terror and violence damaged their individuality and their dignity. Most of the women are not interested to talk about their health conditions; they suffer alienation. Central or State governments are not providing sufficient healing measures to Pandit woman.

Stress Syndromes affected woman's future

In all the migrant camps there were persons with cases of Cardio Vascular Stress Hypertension, Coronary artery disease – angina and heart attacks. According to state medical reports Hypertension created problems in hearts and it leads to heart disease. In Purkhoo camp, Jihri camp and Mishriwala camp, the migrants revealed that In 2008-2009 they lost more than 248 lives due to these diseases.

Psycho trauma– The genocide of the Pandits leads to anxiety, panic attacks and depression, post-traumatic stress syndrome, sleep disorders and nightmares etc.

Endocrine stress–The exiled Pandits became victims of Stress Diabetes, thyroid disorders, ovarian failure leading to premature menopause problems.

Stress (Epidemic) Diabetes

Among all refugee females14.2% (below 30 years) 6%, (31-45 years) 18% are facing stress problems. The important causes are Stress – physical (hyperkinetic stress) and mental, Urbanization and lifestyle changes due to exile.

Climatic unmaking of incipient diabetes – sweet and sugared drinks to fight off heat and exhaustion, Candida infections and boils, preoccupation with health (life is all that is left and to which we cling hard) Awareness of diabetes, detection drive, Genetic predilection.

High death rate

Premature ageing and premature death, Unnatural death, High incidence of serious and potentially fatal diseases, Affliction with Multiple disease syndromes, Poor medical aid, Economic bankruptcy, all leads to lack of desire to live.

Low birth rate

Pandits women remained family planning enthusiasts with one or two child. Exile has brought it to one or none, Late marriage, late conception, Premature menopause and reduced fertility span, diminished libido and hypo-sexuality of exile, Forced celibacy and sexual deprivation, Contraception, Elective abortion.

Kasmir militancy destroyed their everlasting hopes and soul. All militants groups try to destroy their envisages about family. Women and children are the worst victims of Pakistan who have sponsored militancy. State health department is not implementing any projects for depressed, silent, poor Kashmiri pandit women's future (Data Collected from Authors survey).

Conclusion

Kashmiri Pandits families were living in Srinagar, Anantanag, Baramullah, Pulwama, Shopian, Badgam and

Kupwara districts of Kashmir valley and were following five thousand years old customs, believes traditions and celebrations. Militancy has placed Kashmiri Pandits on the crossroads. They took shelter in Dharma Salas, temples and in private rooms along with their relations. Many of them went beyond Jammu, North, South and East and west of India. Delhi became the hub of KP migrants. They feel shy to call them as refugees in their own land. The basic Human Right like right to and the pursuit of happiness is denied in the case of Pandits. The dignity of the individual is ignored; women and children who are the weaker segments and deserve protection were attacked. It is a savage battle that the community is fighting for shelter, livelihood, education, health care, employment and above all for its survival. It is heading towards unmitigated disaster as the deprivation hurt and humiliation have worked havoc on the physical, psychological and mental well-being of the community and have taken a huge toll of its women. The community continues to perish while the nation looks on unconcerned. Many lives have been lost due to starvation, malnutrition, disease and accidents than due to militant bullets. The community is facing dispersal and extinction. The long to return to their homes and hearths, to till their own land, pursue their own professional calling and visit their Gods and temples; but all doors are closed to them.

Bibilography

- Pandit RS, River of Kings, Magna, Bombay, 1963.
- Kaul RU, The Wail of Kashmir, Sterling, New Delhi, 1999.
- Bhatt S, Kashmiri Pandits a Cultural Heritage, Lancers, New Delhi 1995.
- Ahamed Feroz, Ethinicity and Politics, Oxford, Karachi, 1998.
- Kapur ML, kingdoms of Kashmir, J&K Publishers, Jammu, 1983.
- Bhattacharjea Ajith, Kashmir: The wounded valley, Oxford, New Delhi, 1994.
- Pream Shankar Jha, Kashmir 1947, Oxford, Delhi, 1996.
- Pant Kusum, The tears of Kashmiri Pandits, Omkar, Jammu, 2009.
- Nelson Thomas, Kashmir the valley of Mystery, CN-Oslo, 2000.

- Data Collected from J&K State Departments.
- Amy Waldan, Kashmir is bleeding, Star, Hong Kong, 2002.
- Tikko Ramesh, The story of Pandits, OM Publishers, Jammu, 2006.
- Data's are collected from author's survey.

7

Women's Mental Health and Stigma

— *G. Umadevi, Rabina Debbarma*

Abstract

Mental health symptoms are still viewed as threatening and uncomfortable. They can often lead on to various forms of exclusion or discrimination- either within social circles or within the workplace. Mental health problems such as depression or schizophrenia are unpredictable, dangerous. Mental health problems came from family members, peers, and teachers. Stigma can pervade the lives of people with mental health problems in many different ways. According to Corrigan (2004), it "diminishes self-esteem and robs people of social opportunities". Two main types of stigma occur with mental health problems, social stigma and self-stigma. Social stigma also called public stigma, refers to the negative stereotype of those with a mental health problem. The stigma attached to mental illness stigma leads to discrimination in the provision of services for physical illness in those who are mentally ill, reproductive health conditions affect women's health and emotional well-being on a daily basis and can range in severity in terms of the impact their condition has on their everyday life. Women especially may be more prone to internalized or self-stigma in which the way that others see them becomes the way they see themselves. This include denied opportunities such as employment or accommodation because of their illness. Reducing mental health stigma for all women is important, stigma has been shown repeatedly to stifle the willingness to see treatment. This article examines mental health stigma, its outcomes and what should be possible to reduce it.

Keywords: *Mental health, Stigma, Gender, Emotional well-being.*

Introduction

Stigma takes place while society labels a person as tainted or much less ideal. Stigma entails three factors; lack of information (lack of knowledge), bad attitudes (prejudice) and people behaving in methods that discourage the stigmatised individual (discrimination). Several health problems are associated with stigma such as cancers, HIV, AIDS and skin problems which include psoriasis. However the stigma associated with intellectual health troubles is particularly excessive and good sized.

The fact that most people have knowledge of a set of stereotypes does not imply that they agree with them. People who are prejudiced, on the other hand, endorse these negative stereotypes and generate negative emotional reactions as a result. In contrast to stereotypes, which are beliefs, prejudicial attitudes involve an evaluative (generally negative) component. Prejudice also yields emotional responses to stigmatized groups. Prejudice, which is fundamentally a cognitive and affective response, leads to discrimination, the behavioural reaction.

Research suggests that self-stigma and fear of rejection by others lead many persons to not pursue life opportunities for themselves. This paper further develops examples of public and self-stigma. In the process, we summarize research on ways of changing the impact of public and self-stigma.

Self-stigma

Depressed women who choose not to seek treatment could believe that their decision can reduce their risk of being socially stigmatized by others. However, this belief can be self-stigmatizing and it exposes women to the serious health and psychosocial burdens of untreated depression. This theoretical understanding of the self-stigma of depression for women draws on the concepts of social distancing, discredited social identity, identity reclassification (Goffman, 1963), self-stigma (Corrigan, 2004) and derived female social identity (Gilligan, 1982). Goffman's central thesis, partially replicated by Rusch, Bodenhausen, Olschewski, and Corrigan (2010), states that the ability of social groups to stigmatize individuals largely depends on the extent to which the group is able to socialize individuals to respond to the group with feelings of shame and avoidant behaviours.

In comparison to gender, the available data provide inconclusive evidence of ethnicity (Rue & Xie, 2009) as a direct influence on depression self-stigma in women. Regardless of ethnicity, being female is a risk factor for depressive illness (Kendler, Kuhn, & Prescott, 2004). Major secondary predictors of women's mental health include role overload, lack of job satisfaction, and inequality at work and in the home (Glynn, Maclean, Forte, & Cohen, 2009). The influence of ethnicity on women's mental health and self stigmatizing beliefs appears primarily to be socially mediated by racial prejudice (Nicolaidis et al., 2010), income (Falconnier, 2010), social barriers to treatment (Ward, Clark, & Heidrich, 2009), health care disparities (Das, Olfson, McCurtis, & Weisman, 2006), health care costs (Ojeda & McGuire, 2006), immigration status (Nadeem et al., 2007), language barriers (Hodgkin, Volpe-Vartanian& Alegria, 2007) and symptom recognition (Epstein et al., 2010).

Public Stigma

Public stigma for people with mental illness (PWMI) is negative evaluative and emotional reactions (prejudice) as well as discrimination (unjust treatment) stemming from beliefs in socially learned stereotypes (Corrigan, 2004; Corrigan, Kerr, & Knudsen, 2005; Corrigan & Watson, 2002; Fox, Earnshaw, Taverna, & Vogt, 2017). The consequences of public stigma are profound, resulting in loss of opportunities and resources (Corrigan et al., 2005). People with mental illness who report perceived (anticipated or internalized) and experienced (Fox et al.,

2017) stigma describe increased emotional distress (Boyd, Adler, Otilingam, & Peters, 2014; Boyd, Otilingam, & DeForge, 2014; Ilic et al., 2013), decreased treatment service use (Kao et al., 2016; Keyes et al., 2010), and diminished quality of life (Alonso et al., 2009; Boyd, Adler et al., 2014; Ilic et al., 2013; Lasalvia et al., 2013).

Sex Differences in Perceptions of Stigma

Studies consistently find that women are more likely to seek help for emotional issues (Moller-Leimkuhler, 2002) and possess more positive attitudes toward counseling than men (Fischer & Farina, 1995). One reason may be that men perceive greater stigma associated with seeking help. Society considers counseling to be a last resort, something to use only after other sources of support have failed (Angermeyer, Matschinger, & Riedel-Heller, 1999). Such attitudes may be particularly salient for men, who are expected to be stoic, controlled, and self-sufficient (Hammen & Peters, 1977). Consistent with this, adolescents are more willing to refer a girl to get help than a boy (Raviv, Sills, Raviv, & Wilansky, 2000). Thus, men may perceive that there is public stigma associated with their seeking help (Timlin-Scalera, Ponterotto, Blumberg, & Jackson, 2003) and believe that they would be stigmatized for discussing certain issues with a counselor (Martin, Wrisberg, Beitel, & Lounsbury, 1997). Similarly, the emphasis of the traditional male gender role on being independent and in control may lead to increased concerns about the loss of self-esteem associated with seeking help, as it may mean admitting to the inability to handle things on one's own (Addis & Mahalik, 2003). Therefore, if a man believed that he needed counseling, he might experience a greater sense of failure, which would make the act of asking for help particularly difficult. Consistent with this, men have been found to experience greater self-stigma than women regarding help seeking in college settings (Vogel et al., 2006).

Stigma and its consequences

Two fundamental forms of stigma arise with intellectual fitness issues, social stigma and self-stigma. Social stigma, also called public stigma, refers to negative stereotypes with a mental health trouble. These stereotypes come to outline the character, mark them out as one of a kind and prevent them being visible as person. Social stigma is associated with discrimination. For instance someone with a mental fitness trouble can also find that others, including pals and associates, avoid them. They may also locate it more difficult to benefit housing, gain employment and get right of entry to healthcare and might locate that their account is much less probable to be believed by the police in the event that they file a crime. A 2011 survey determined that nearly nine out of ten mental health carrier customers in England had experienced discrimination. The results of discrimination, as an instance unemployment and social isolation, can stigmatise someone further. Self-stigma occurs when someone internalises terrible stereotypes. This can motive low vanity, shame and hopelessness. Both sorts of stigma can lead a person to avoid looking for assist for their intellectual health trouble due to embarrassment or fear of being shunned or rejected. When this happens the underlying trouble can go untreated causing needless suffering. A postpone in receiving treatment can get worse the outlook of some situations as can the pressure and tension due to experiencing stigma. Family individuals can become stigmatised by way of a relative having a mental health trouble, so known as courtesy stigma.

Lack of knowledge and negative attitudes

The level of knowledge among the public regarding mental health problems is poor and negative beliefs and attitudes are widespread. Both are the key elements of stigma. One of the most common and damaging misperceptions is that people with schizophrenia are violent and a danger to others. This view has been perpetuated by misleading media reports. Research shows that although schizophrenia is associated with violent behaviour this accounts for less than 10% of violent crime in society. A person with schizophrenia is far more likely to be the victim of violence than to be violent to another person. They are also more likely to be the victim of violence than a person in the general population. If a person with schizophrenia becomes aggressive this is often related to the use of excessive alcohol or street drugs which is similar to the situation seen with people who do not suffer from schizophrenia but become aggressive.

Public surveys show that eating disorders and problematic use of alcohol and other drugs are frequently seen as an individual's own fault People with these disorders, and also depression and anxiety, are often viewed as needing to 'pull themselves together'. Such views would rarely be associated with cancer or heart disease. In reality the cause of most mental health problems, like most physical health problems, is complex and multiple risk factors contribute. Some factors can be modified which is important as it gives people some control over their health, for example eating a healthy diet to reduce the risk of heart disease or ensuring a sensible work/life balance to reduce the risk of depression. However many risk factors for physical and mental health problems are beyond an individual's control, for example inheriting an increased vulnerability to develop heart disease, depression or some other medical condition. Another example of a risk factor, beyond the control of the sufferer, is childhood abuse and neglect which increases the risk for develop depression, problematic use of alcohol and other drugs, eating disorders, personality disorder and psychosis in later life.

Other misperceptions include the view that mental health problems are uncommon, that sufferers seldom recover and that treatment is ineffective. Mental health problems are common; one in four adults will suffer from a mental health problem in any given year and mental health problems account for about one third of all general practitioner (GP) consultations. However these disorders have a far better outcome many people realise. For example half of those affected with a depressive illness recover within three months. Long term studies show that many people diagnosed with schizophrenia are functioning well and at least one in ten people who experience a first psychotic episode will not experience a further episode. A minority of people with mental health problems have severe, long-term symptoms and experience significant disability but this is no different to the situation with many physical illnesses. Most people who are treated for a mental health problem receive all their care from their GP and other staff in primary care with about 10% receiving additional help from specialist psychiatric services such as community mental health teams. Treatment depends on the nature of the problem and the individual. However, in general both talking treatments, such as cognitive behavioural treatment (CBT), and medication are reasonably effective. Many mental health problems can be treated successfully with talking treatments alone but medication is an important part of the treatment for many more severe problems. When medication is given it should always be accompanied by psychological and social approaches. The effectiveness of psychiatric drugs in a range of psychiatric conditions is similar to the effectiveness of medical drugs in a range of physical health disorders including migraine, heart failure, chronic obstructive pulmonary disease and high blood pressure.

Negative views of mental health problems are held by people in all walks of life and of all ages. People with mental health problems can experience stigma and discrimination from family members, friends, teachers, work colleagues and health professionals including GPs, psychiatrists and psychiatric nurses.

Strategies for Changing Public Stigma

Change strategies for public stigma have been grouped into three approaches: protest, education, and contact. Groups protest inaccurate and hostile representations of mental illness as a way to challenge the stigmas they represent. These efforts send two messages. To the media: STOP reporting inaccurate representations of mental illness. To the public: STOP believing negative views about mental illness. Wahl believes citizens are encountering far fewer sanctioned examples of stigma and stereotypes because of protest efforts. Anecdotal evidence suggests that protest campaigns have been effective in getting stigmatizing images of mental illness withdrawn. There is, however, little empirical research on the psychological impact of protest campaigns on stigma and discrimination, suggesting an important direction for future research. Protest is a reactive strategy; it attempts to diminish negative attitudes about mental illness, but fails to promote more positive attitudes that are supported by facts. Education provides information so that the public can make more informed decisions about mental illness. This approach to changing stigma has been most thoroughly examined by investigators. Research, for example, has suggested that persons who evince a better understanding of mental illness are less likely to endorse stigma and discrimination. Hence, the strategic provision of information about mental illness seems to lessen negative stereotypes. Several studies have shown that participation in education programs on mental illness led to improved attitudes about persons with these problem. Education programs are effective for a wide variety of participants, including college undergraduates, graduate students, adolescents, community residents, and persons with mental illness. Stigma is further diminished when members of the general public meet persons with mental illness who are able to hold down jobs or live as good neighbours in the community. Research has shown an inverse relationship between having contact with a person with mental illness and endorsing psychiatric stigma. Hence, opportunities for the public to meet persons with severe mental illness may discount stigma. Interpersonal contact is further enhanced when the general public is able to regularly interact with people with mental illness as peers.

Reducing stigma

Education campaigns can help reduce stigma. Most are targeted at the general public but they can also focus on specific groups, for example teachers, the police or medical students. 'Time to Change' is England's largest mental health anti-stigma campaign and was launched in 2009. It is led by the mental health charities Mind and Rethink Mental Illness and is funded by the Department of Health, the Big Lottery Fund and Comic Relief. Education campaigns often involve individuals with a mental health problem telling their personal story, either through film clips or face to face in workshops, with an emphasis on hope and recovery. Such 'social contact intervention' is an effective way to reduce stigma. Providing accurate information and key messages is also important. Examples of key messages include that mental health problems are common and affect people of all ages, backgrounds and cultures but are not a barrier to living a fulfilling and successful life as shown by the many famous people who have suffered from depression and other psychiatric problems.

Educational campaigns often target the media to try and ensure a more balanced and accurate coverage of mental health issues. This is crucial as the media can perpetuate negative stereotypes through inaccurate and distorted reporting of news stories. Surveys of newspapers in England find that just under half of articles with a mental health theme are stigmatising, for example they use pejorative language or emphasise the risk of violence to others.

The fictional portrayal of people with mental health problems in cinema and television is often misleading and stigmatising. A recent report identified four main cinematic stereotypes of people with mental health problems; objects of fun and ridicule, fakers, people to be pitied or violent individuals. The last portrayal is closely linked to cinematic portrayals of psychosis. The media reflect society's existing prejudices and cannot be blamed for the existence of stigma but these representations have been described as a 'reservoir' that perpetuates damaging stereotypes. On the other hand some depictions of mental illness, particularly in several recent television dramas, are accurate, positive and can help reduce stigma and increase public understanding.

Tackling stigma is not only the responsibility of those organising large scale education campaigns. A 'bottom up' approach is also needed. People who have suffered from a mental health problem, family members, health care professionals and the general public need to feel confident to challenge negative stereotypes that they encounter, whether at work or socially. An example of this occurring on a large scale was in 2003 when the Sun newspaper reported on the former world heavyweight champion boxer Frank Bruno being admitted to a psychiatric ward with the headline *'Bonkers Bruno Locked Up'*. There was an immediate outcry by members of the public and mental health charities and the paper was forced to change the headline to the more sympathetic *'Sad Bruno In Mental Home'* for the second edition.

Another way to combat stigma is through anti-discrimination policy and legislation. This approach has proven successful in reducing discrimination experienced by people on grounds of gender, race and sexual orientation. The Equality Act 2010 made it unlawful in Great Britain to discriminate directly or indirectly against someone who has a disability in work, education, public services and several other specified situations. The Act defines a disability as a physical or mental impairment that has a 'substantial' and 'long-term' negative effect on a person's ability to carry out normal day-to-day activities. Long-term means the disorder has lasted a year, or is likely to last at least a year, or is likely to be recurrent. As such the definition could include people with a wide range of mental health problems such as learning difficulties, depression, schizophrenia and bipolar disorder. The Act also requires employers to make reasonable adjustments in the work place if a person's disability puts them at a disadvantage compared to others.

Conclusions

Researchers are beginning to apply what social psychologists have learned about prejudice and stereotypes in general to the stigma related to mental illness. We have made progress in understanding the dimensions of mental illness stigma, and the processes by which public stereotypes are translated into discriminatory behaviour. At the same time, we are beginning to develop models of self-stigma, which is a more complex phenomenon than originally assumed. The models developed thus far need to be tested on various sub-populations, including different ethnic groups and power-holders (legislators, judges, police officers, health care providers, employers, landlords). We are also learning about stigma change strategies. Contact in particular seems to be effective for changing individual attitudes. Researchers need to examine whether changes resulting from anti-stigma interventions are maintained over time. All of the research discussed in this paper examines stigma at the individual psychological level. For the most part, these studies have ignored the fact that stigma is inherent in the social structures that make up society. Stigma is evident in the way laws, social services, and the justice system are structured as well as ways in which resources are allocated. Research that focuses on the social structures that maintain stigma and strategies for changing them is sorely needed.

References

- Ciftci, A., Jones, N., & Corrigan, P. W. (2013). Mental health stigma in the Muslim community. *Journal of Muslim Mental Health*, 7(1).
- Koller, M., & Stuart, H. (2016). Reducing stigma in high school youth. *Acta Psychiatrica Scandinavica*, 134, 63-70.
- Khan, N., Kausar, R., Khalid, A., & Farooq, A. (2015). Gender differences among discrimination & stigma experienced by depressive patients in Pakistan. *Pakistan journal of medical sciences*, 31(6), 1432.
- Parcesepe, A. M., & Cabassa, L. J. (2013). Public stigma of mental illness in the United States: a systematic literature review. *Administration and Policy in Mental Health and Mental Health Services Research*, 40(5), 384-399.
- Pedersen, E. R., & Paves, A. P. (2014). Comparing perceived public stigma and personal stigma of mental health treatment seeking in a young adult sample. *Psychiatry research*, 219(1), 143-150.
- Van Der Sanden, R. L., Bos, A. E., Stutterheim, S. E., Pryor, J. B., & Kok, G. (2015). Stigma by association among family members of people with a mental illness: A qualitative analysis. *Journal of Community & Applied Social Psychology*, 25(5), 400-417.
- Wirth, J. H., & Bodenhausen, G. V. (2009). The role of gender in mental-illness stigma: A national experiment. *Psychological Science*, 20(2), 169-173

8

Women's perspectives on Quality of Maternal Health care Services: A study of Government Maternity Hospitals in Hyderabad

— *Ishrat Batool Naik*

Abstract

A healthy child needs a healthy mother. According to the United Nations Children's Fund (UNICEF), at least 20% of the disease burden in children under 5 is related to problems in maternal health and malnutrition, as well as the quality of care at delivery and during the newborn period. Moreover, according to UNICEF, a baby whose mother dies during childbirth is less likely to survive, and children who lost their mothers are 10 times more likely to die within two years of the death of their mothers. The care of the mother has to be intensive, not only in prenatal care but also postpartum. The mother needs to be well, both physically and mentally, to take good care of her child. Mothers are also fundamental to ensure the health and quality of the lives of children. According to the World Health Organization (WHO), mothers are the main providers of care such as nutrition, oral health and psychological health. Clemente says. "If the mother is not well, how will she ever take this child to the physiotherapist or the neurologist, or follow doctor. Thus, the main aim of the present article is to explore the Perspectives of Women on quality Health care services and what problems they are facing during pregnancy and all that. For this study, the investigators contacted 150 Mother respondents on a random sampling basis in three government maternity hospitals of Hyderabad. An Interview schedule was used as a tool of data collection for illiterate respondents while the questionnaire was used for educated respondents. The study indicates that Mothers faced work pressure during pregnancy due to the joint family system. Most of the respondents were facing health problems during pregnancy due to non-availability of female doctors, insufficient clinical and non-clinical facilities and unawareness of different government schemes.

Keywords: *Health Problems. Maternal Health, Malnutrition, Work pressure.*

1.1 Introduction

"No matter where a woman lives, giving birth should be a time of joy, not a sentence to death."

— Thoraya Ahmed Obaid

(Former Executive Director of UNFPA, 2001–2010)

In the lives of women of reproductive age, Pregnancy and motherhood are natural processes. These processes are generally considered to be positive and fulfilling experiences. However, for various reasons many women die during pregnancy, childbirth and the post-partum period. Improving maternal health and reducing maternal mortality are accepted as human rights challenges and these issues have been emphasized in several international declarations and national policies. Enhanced scientific knowledge and availability of modern technology have brought several significant victories in global health over the past five decades but maternal mortality reduction remains a serious challenge in majority of low- and middle-income countries.

India has a huge toll of maternal deaths, with 50,000 deaths in 2013, which constituted 17% of the global burden of maternal mortality. It has achieved a significant decline in the Maternal Mortality Ratio (MMR) from 892 maternal deaths/100,000 live births in 1972–76 to 178 in 2010-12. Nevertheless, the country is still far away from reducing it to 109 maternal deaths per 100,000 live births, which is the Millennium Development Goal (MDG) 5 target for the country. Improving maternal health and reducing maternal mortality are not simply health issues; rather they are critical human rights issues. The United Nations Human Rights Council (UNHRC) accepted, in 2009, that preventable maternal mortality is a human rights challenge, and especially the right to life and to enjoy the highest attainable standard of physical and mental health, including sexual and reproductive health.

In recent years the attention of global and national health experts has been drawn to the seemingly intractable scourge of maternal and newborn mortality in low and middle-income countries (LMICs). Every year 287,000 to 350,000 women die due to pregnancy or childbirth complications, and about a million babies die during delivery – these are fresh stillborn babies who were alive at the onset of labour and minutes prior to delivery. In addition, approximately 9 million newborns die before their fifth birthdays and about 40 per cent of these die in the 28 days after birth. At the beginning of the century, world leaders agreed on the Millennium Development Goals (MDGs); a package of indicators and targets that countries voluntarily set for themselves. The fourth and fifth MDGs focus on the reduction of child mortality by two-thirds and maternal mortality by three-quarters respectively between 1990 and 2015 [4, 9].

Healthy Motherhood not only benefits the newborn but influences the global and national development (Fraser A. et al 2004). The international conference on population and development (ICPD), 1994 has stressed on the importance of women's health and especially reproductive health for overall development. For long the International Health Community and National Health Planners, have directed their efforts towards increasing the coverage of maternal care (antenatal, delivery and postnatal) but less attention has been directed to the content of the program. As a result, data indicative of high coverage of care were commonly coexisting with high levels of maternal and neonatal morbidity and mortality (WHO, 1994).

1.2 Purpose of the Study

The main purpose of the present study is to explore the Perspectives of Women on quality Health care services and the problems they are facing during pregnancy. It also tries to investigate the complication which mothers faced at the time of delivery and to what extent the respondents are availing clinical and non-clinical facilities in government hospitals.

1.3 Methodology

The present study is descriptive in nature and the survey research method was found suitable for the study. A random sample of 150 Mothers from three maternity hospital of Hyderabad (namely Gandhi Hospital, Modern Govt. Maternity Hospital Afzal Gang and Govt. Modern Maternity Hospital Koti) were drawn for the study. For the purpose of data collection, the investigators used Self-Constructed questionnaire along with the observation schedule. The data were analyzed using descriptive statistics (Mean and percentage).

1.4 Results

Table 8.1: Health Problems during Pregnancy

Sl. No.	*Problems faced by Mothers*	*Respondents*	*Percentage*
1.	Anaemia	150	**100**
2.	Depression	12	**8**
3.	UTI	13	**8.66**
4.	BP	62	**41.33**
5.	Preterm-labor	11	**7.33**
6.	Diabetes	8	**5.33**
7.	Placenta Abruption	8	**4.66**

Multi-response table

Analysis and Interpretation

Table No 8.1shows that 100% of respondents are travail with anaemia. Apart from that 41% of respondents are facing blood pressure, 9% UTI, 8% depression, 7% preterm labor, 5% diabetes and 5% of respondents are suffering from placenta abruption. From the above analyses, it can be concluded that during pregnancy women are comfronting with several health problems. If these problems were not alleviated on time it will not only effect the woman but also newborn. It may also lead to loss of lives of the mother or her child. It is necessary to take precautions and provide healthy nutritious food in pregnancy period so that both the mother and her child may be healthy.

Table 8.2: Complications at the time of Delivery

BP	*Loss of water*	*No labor pain*	*Preterm Delivery*	*Prolonged-Delivery*	*Total*
62 (41.33)	27 (18%)	25 (16.66%)	17 (11.33%)	19 (12.66%)	150 (100%)

Analysis and Interpretation

Table No 8.2 shows that 41% respondents faced the complications of blood pressure at the time of delivery, 18% challenged water loss, 17% feels no labor pain and then they have to meet cesarean, 13% confronted with prolonged delivery and 11% respondents were facing preterm delivery.

From the above table and analysis, it can be inferred that majority of respondents are facing many complications at the time of delivery where only a few respondents face fewer complications or having normal delivery either in the home or in hospitals.

Table 8.3: Clinical facilities available in Government Hospitals

Sl. No	Facilities	*Gandhi Hospital*		*Modern Govt. Maternity Hospital*		*Govt. Modern Maternity Hospital Koti*		*Total*	
		Yes	*No*	*Yes*	*No*	*Yes*	*No*	*Yes*	*No*
1	**Medicines**	30 (60)	20 (40)	22 (44)	28 (56)	21 (42)	29 (58)	73 (49)	77 (51)
2	**Operation Theatre**	47 (94)	3 (6)	45 (90)	5 (10)	43 (86)	7 (14)	135 (90)	15 (10)
3	**Newborn Care**	30 (60)	20 (40)	33 (66)	17 (34)	36 (72)	14 (28)	61 (41)	89 (59)
4	**Infection care**	23 (46)	27 (54)	13 (26)	37 (74)	20 (40)	30 (60)	56 (37)	94 (63)
5	**Sick newborn care unit**	39 (78)	11 (22)	8 (16)	42 (84)	10 (20)	40 (80)	57 (38)	93 (62)
6	**Blood Bank**	10 (20)	40 (80)	13 (26)	37 (74)	15 (30)	35 (70)	38 (25).	112 (76)
7	**Instruments**	42 (84)	8 (16)	39 (78)	11 (22)	44 (88)	6 (12)	125 (83)	25 (17)
Total		**221 (63)**	**129 (37)**	**173 (49)**	**177 (51)**	**189 (54)**	**161 (46)**	**545 (52)**	**505 (48)**

Analysis and Interpretation

Table No 8.3 provides information about available clinical amenities in hospitals. Generally, it shows that 52% of respondents are of the opinion that there are facilities available in hospitals; where 48% are of the view that no adequate clinical facilities are existing in hospitals. When the data was analyzed in-hospital wise differently, it was found that majority of the respondents (63%) of Gandhi Hospital are availing the clinical amenities; whereas in Modern government maternity and government maternity hospital Koti only 49% and 54% respondents respectively are accessing these facilities.

From the above analysis, it can be inferred that even today government hospitals are lacking the basic clinical amenities. In one hand govt. are making programs and policies about maternal and child health care but on the other hand, common people are not able to take advantages of these programs and policies. There are many causes behind this cavity, for example, negligence or non-seriousness of hospital administration, people are not aware of these facilities, the unconcerned behaviour of ASHA, non-implementation or late execution of these policies or facilities etc.

During Survey it was found that there is a worthy arrangement of some clinical facilities such as Operation theatre and equipment in hospitals. Whereas, there are absence and unavailability of other clinical facilities such as blood bank (such as in Gandhi Hospital, Modern Maternity Hospital and Govt. Maternity Hospital despite having availability of blood the patients are not able to receive or having access to it. Either these patient are denying by providing blood or the matching type blood is not available there), sick newborn care, newborn care unit and infection care in different hospitals.

Table 8.4: Non-Clinical facilities available in Government Hospitals

Sl. No.	*Facilities*	*Gandhi Hospital*		*Modern Govt. Maternity Hospital*		*Govt. Modern Maternity Hospital Koti*		*Total*	
		Yes	*No*	*Yes*	*No*	*Yes*	*No*	*Yes*	*No*
1.	**Beds**	46 (92)	4 (8)	38 (76)	12 (24)	37 (74)	13 (26)	121 (81)	29 (19)
2.	**Sanitation**	15 (30)	35 (70)	38 (76)	12 (24)	39 (78)	11 (22)	92 (61)	58 (39)
3.	**Water**	37 (74)	13 (26)	29 (58)	21 (42)	11 (22)	39 (78)	77 (51)	73 (49)
4.	**Electricity**	32 (64)	18 (36)	35 (70)	15 (30)	33 (66)	17 (34)	100 (67)	50 (33)
5.	**Ambulance**	33 (66)	17 (34)	17 (34)	33 (66)	27 (54)	23 (46)	77 (51)	73 (49)
Total		**163 (65)**	**87 (35)**	**157 (63)**	**93 (37)**	**147 (59)**	**103 (41)**	**467 (62)**	**283 (38)**

Analysis and Interpretation

Table No. 8.4 provides information about available non-clinical facilities in hospitals. Generally, it was found that majority of respondents 63% are of the opinion that there are non-clinical facilities available in hospitals; where 37% are of the view that no adequate non-clinical services are prevailing in hospitals. When the data was analyzed in-hospital wise differently, it was found that majority of the respondents (63%) of Gandhi Hospital are availing the clinical amenities; whereas in Modern government maternity and government maternity hospital Koti only 49% and 54% respondents respectively are accessing these facilities. In terms of availability of beds, electricity and ambulances Gandhi hospital is ahead of the other two hospitals whereas govt. maternity hospital is ahead of the other two hospitals in terms of availability of water facility. The important fact which arises here is that in all the three hospitals there is no sufficient arrangement of hygiene and sanitation which is necessary for pregnant women.

During the survey it was observed that in Hyderabad hospitals due to scarce of sanitation the patient wards are racked with dust and different insects which result in infection in newborn babies and their mothers.

1.5 Major Findings

I. Majority of the respondents are facing more than one health problems during pregnancy such as Anemia, blood pressure, UTI, depression, preterm labor, diabetes and placenta abruption.

II. Most respondents (41%) were facing complication of blood pressure at the time delivery.

III. Out of 150 respondents, 78 were of the opinion that sufficient clinical facilities are available in hospitals whereas, 72 respondents say no adequate clinical facilities are existing in hospitals.

IV. Majority of the respondents 95 out of 150 were of the opinion that sufficient non-clinical facilities are available in hospitals whereas, 45 respondents say no adequate nonclinical facilities are existing in hospitals.

1.5 Discussion and Conclusion

India has shown good progress in the MDGs' era and narrowly missed its MDG 4 target for under-five mortality, achieving an under-five mortality rate of 43 per 1000 against the target of 42 per 1000 live births. However, in spite of these gains, the burden still remains high with India contributing to one-fifth of under-five mortality burden and a quarter of neonatal deaths globally. In terms of absolute numbers, this translates into 1.1 million under 5 deaths, of which 630,000 happen during the first four weeks of life. The states of Uttar Pradesh, Madhya Pradesh, Rajasthan and Bihar contribute to more than half of newborn and under-five deaths in India. The major causes of newborn deaths in India are pre-maturity/preterm (35 per cent); neonatal infections (33 per cent); intrapartum-related complications/ birth asphyxia (20 per cent); and congenital malformations (9 per cent). Most newborn deaths are preventable by improving quality of care during delivery and care at birth. Simple interventions like skilled birth attendance and access to emergency obstetric care can reduce NMR by 41 per cent while early initiation of breastfeeding can reduce NMR by per cent.

As the lead technical partner in the country for Newborn and Child Health, UNICEF has been involved from the beginning of the Integrated Management of Newborn and Childhood Illness (IMNCI) programme in India. It has also played a key role in strengthening Facility Based Newborn Care (FBNC) in the country in line with increasing institutional delivery, scaling up the model of Special Newborn Care Units (SNCUs) that were first piloted by UNICEF with the Government of West Bengal in Purulia district. The SNCU online monitoring developed by UNICEF in Madhya Pradesh has been adopted by the Government of India for national scale-up. In February 2013, policymakers joined leaders from the private sector and civil society in Mahabalipuram, Tamil Nadu for India's Call to Action – 'Child Survival and Development for Every

Child in India.' Convened under the banner of A Promise Renewed, the high-level forum launched the 'Strategic Approach to Reproductive Maternal Newborn Child and Adolescent Health,' an ambitious roadmap for accelerating child survival and development.

The government is making steady progress implementing this bold strategy, which identifies 184 high-priority districts across some of the country's poorest states. With the support of partners, including UNICEF, USAID, the Bill & Melinda Gates Foundation, UNFPA, the Norway India Partnership Initiative and the Government of the United Kingdom, the Government of India is developing strategies for bridging and financing health care gaps in the priority districts, and implementing a system for monitoring and reviewing local-level health care services.

References

- WHO, UNICEF, UNFPA, World Bank, United Nations Population Division: Trends in maternal mortality:1990 to 2013- Estimates by WHO, UNICEF, UNFPA, World Bank and United Nations Population Division. Geneva: World Health Organization; 2014.
- Registrar General of India: Special Bulletin on Maternal Mortality in India 2010-2012. New Delhi: Office of the Registrar General of India; 2013.
- United Nations Human Rights Council: Resolution 11/8. Preventable maternal mortality and morbidity and human rights, dated 17 June 2009. New York: United Nations; 2009.
- United-Nations. Millennium Development Goals: Target 5A. 2013 November 27, 2013; Available from: http://www.un.org/ millenniumgoals/ maternal.shtml.
- Hogan, M.C., et al., Maternal mortality for 181 countries, 1980–2008: a systematic analysis of progress towards Millennium Development Goal 5. The Lancet, 2010. 375(9726): p. 16091623.
- Lawn, J., K. Shibuya, and C. Stein, No cry at birth: global estimates of intrapartum stillbirths and intrapartum-related neonatal deaths. Bulletin of the World Health Organization, 2005. 83(6): p. 409-417.
- UNICEF, The State of the World's Children Special Edition: Celebrating 20 Years of the Convention on the Rights of the Child, 2009: New York. p. 18.

- Lozano, R., et al., Progress towards Millennium Development Goals 4 and 5 on maternal and child mortality: an updated systematic analysis. The Lancet, 2011. 378(9797): p. 11391165.
- United-Nations. Millennium Development Goal: Target 4A. 2013 November 27, 2013; Available from: http://www.un.org/millenniumgoals/childhealth.shtml.
- Jat, T. R. (2014). Maternal health and health care in Madhya Pradesh state of India: an exploration using a human rights lens. Umea University Medical Dissertations, Sweden: Umea www.phmed.umu.se
- http://unicef.in/Whatwedo/2/Neonatal-Health- 23/11/17

9

Management of Menstrual Problems in Siddha System

— **Dr. M. Siva,**
Dr. M. Thiruthani

Abstract

Siddha system is a very effective and ancient system in this modern world. It deals the siddha aspect of management of menstrual problems in women's life. In siddha medical text book referred the "Siddha Materia medica" reveals management of menstrual problems in women's life. In this research, the following various methods of siddha treatment were applied for the various problems occurred in the women's menstrual cycle like menorrhagia, dysmenorrhoea, and amenorrhoea. The methods of siddha treatment including internal and external medicines are having excellent result. In this research menorrhagia recorded as 37 raw materials and internal medicine were extremely noted. In plant raw materials are Fabaceae(6) and Anacardiaceae, Malvaceae, Moraceae, Poaceae are occupied 2 times, which families are most occupied among 28 families. 34 type of internal medicine and 03 type of external medicine were noted. In internal medicine kudineer(16), karkam(4), legiyum(2) were most occupied. In external medicine peechu(2) were most time noted. In Dysmenorrhoea recorded as 18 raw materials and internal medicine were extremely noted. In plant raw materials are occupied Fabaceae(2), Loganaceae(2), Solanaceae (2) among 15 families. In internal medicine kudineeer(5), chooranam(3),charu(3) were mostly occupied and external medicine thylam were noted 3 times. In amenorrhoea 10 raw materials were recorded. This raw materials occupied in 10 families. Internal medicine kudineer(5), karkam(2), charu(2) are most time occupied. In external medicine pattru (application) is noted. Finally ***concluded*** *as siddha medical system dealing with management of menstrual problems in women's life at ancient time which management protocols should be established with proper scientific evidence based in future for man - kind purpose world.*

Key words: *menorrhagia, dysmenorrhoea, amenorrhoea, siddha management, siddha materiamedica*

I. Introduction

Menstruation, is the periodical flow of blood from the uterus through the cervix and out through the vagina, and it is also called a "period". Monthly menstrual periods are a normal part of a woman's life. Menstruation is essential for the renewal of the uterine lining in preparation for pregnancy. The process of degeneration of endometrial bed and removal of the same though vagina occurs at regular interval and is called the menstrual cycle. The menstrual cycle provides important body chemicals, called hormones, to keep healthy. It also prepares body for pregnancy each month.

The initiation of menstruation is an important milestone in the reproductive lives of women. Menstruation is the end point in a series of events which begins in the cerebral cortex and hypothalamus and ends at the uterus in the hypothalamic - pituitary – ovarian – uterine axis. Any break in this axis creates menstrual problems. Excessive in appropriately timed menstruation and amenorrhoea are the most common complaints for which women seek advice from medical health care providers. Abnormalmen struation can be a harbinger of a sinister pelvic pathology are denote a relatively minor problem; therefore, a thorough investigation into the problem is called for in every patient presenting with this complaint. In normal healthy women, menarche occurs between the age of 10 and 16 years, mean age of, menarche of being around 12.5 years. Cyclic menstruation persists throughout the reproductive era of life with an average rhythm of 28 ± 7 days, inclusive of4-6 days of bleeding (except pregnancy and lactation). It is not uncommon for minor variation to occur from time to time.

Menstrual symptoms

Common symptoms include, breast swelling and tenderness, tension, bloating, acne breakouts, leg, back, or stomach cramping. **Premenstrual syndrome** This is very common condition can include symptoms such as, rapid changes in mood, insomnia, dizziness, bloating, social withdrawal, difficulty in concentrating, breast tenderness, tiredness etc.

Various types of menstrual cycle irregularities present in women's life that is amenorrhoea, oligomenorrhoea, polymenorrhoea, menorrhagia, metrorrhagia, menometrorrhagia, hypo menorrhoea, intermenstrual, precocious, postcoital bleeding. **Menorrhagia** denotes regularly timed episodes of bleeding that are excessive in amount (>80ml) and/ or duration of flow (>5 days). **Dysmenorrhoea** means cramping pain accompanying menstruation. **Amenorrhoea** indicates the absence of menstruation. It is a symptom and not a disease entity.

Menorrhagia

Menorrhagia is defined as menstruation at regular cycle intervals but with excessive flow and duration and is one of the most common gynecologic complaints in contemporary gynecology. Clinically, menorrhagia is defined as total blood loss exceeding 80 mL per cycle [13] or menses lasting longer than 7 days.

Symptoms

The signs and symptoms of Menorrhagia include, Anemia, Weakness and fatigue, Soaking through one or more sanitary pads or tampons every hour, usage of more than one sanitary pads to control the flow, needing to change the sanitary protection frequently, especially during the night, menstrual cycles last for more than a week, presence of blood clots in the menstrual flow, Inability to complete daily tasks due to heavy bleeding.

Causes

Hormonal imbalance, loss of ovarian function, presence of fibroids in the uterus (Small growth on the uterus lining), usage of Intrauterine device (IUD), pregnancy complications, uterine cancer, ovarian cancer, cervical, inherited bleeding disorders, anti-inflammatory medications, pelvic inflammatory disease (PID), thyroid problems, liver or kidney diseases.

Dysmenorrhoea

Dysmenorrhoea refers to excessive pain with menstruation. Whilst pain is frequently considered a normal symptom in the menstrual cycle, excessive pain or pain which leads to decreased ability to carry out normal daily activities is abnormal. The degree of pain that may be tolerated by individuals varies greatly and thus dysmenorrhoea is a highly subjective disorder.

Types of Dysmenorrhoea

There are two types of dysmenorrhoea - primary and secondary. Primary refers to pain which has no obvious cause. It tends to occur in younger women with no pelvic abnormality, particularly in the first few years after menarche (the period during which menstruation begins) Secondary dysmenorrhoea refers to pain which arises as a result of an underlying condition. It usually begins in older women in the third or fourth decade.

Signs and Symptoms

Symptoms experienced with dysmenorrhoea depend on whether you have primary or secondary dysmenorrhoea. Pain is the predominant feature in both types, cramp-like pain in lower back, abdomen and inner thighs, tight sensation in inner thighs, nausea, vomiting, diarrhea, light headedness.

Amanorrhoea

Amanorrhoea is the absence of menstrual periods in a woman during her reproductive years (after the age of puberty but before the typical age of the menopause). Amanorrhoea is classified as either 'primary' (menstrual periods not having started by age 16 years) or 'secondary', which is the absence of menstrual periods in a woman who has previously been menstruating for six months or more. Amanorrhoea may be caused by many factors, including, defects in one or more areas of the reproductive system, such as the hypothalamus and pituitary gland (parts of the brain regulating reproduction), ovaries, uterus or vagina, a side-effect from treatment for cancer, a symptom of endometrial cancer.

Causes of Amanorrhoea

Hypothalamus

Eating disorders, excessive exercise, high levels of prolonged physical or mental stress, brain tumour, following brain surgery or injury.

Anterior pituitary

Pituitary tumour (eg prolactinoma), following brain surgery or injury, metabolic diseases such as haemochromatosis.

Ovary

Genetic abnormality preventing normal ovarian function, premature ovarian failure, when the ovary goes into 'menopause' at an early age (may affect 1 in 10 000 women by the age of 20), polycystic ovarian syndrome.

Uterus

Pregnancy, abnormal uterus, lack of uterus, Abnormalities of the outflow tract:, imperforate hymen causes an outflow obstruction, transverse vaginal septum can be anywhere along the tract between the hymenal ring and cervix, vaginal or cervical abnormality.

II. AIM

- To enumerate the number of plants used in management of menstrual problems (Menorrhagia, Dysmenorrhoea, Amenorrhoea) siddha maleria medical.

Objective

- To list out the number of plants which are indicate to management of menstrual problems in Siddha Medicine.
- To make the solution against of menstrual problems.
- To take awareness of menstrual problems about women's.
- To ensure the relationship between women's health and our siddha system.

III. Materials and Methods

- **Research type –** Literature Review
- **Data collected from** – "Siddha materiamedica", - a translation of Tamil siddha text gunapadam-mooligai written by Vaidya Rathnam K. S. Murugesa Muthalitar, Edited by: Dr. Anaivaari R. Anandan, published by: Department of Indian Medicine & Homeopathy, Chennai 600 106, 1st edition - 1936, reprinted Year – 2013.
- **Analysis**

  - Data analysis by MS excel.

  - Descriptive simple Statistical way.

Results

Menorrhagia

Plant name	*Botanical name*	*Family*	*Type of plant*	*Part used*	*Type of medicine*	*Formulation of medicine*
Asoku	***Saracaasoca***	Fabaceae	Tree	Pattai	Internal	Charu
Aththi	***Ficusracemosa***	Moraceae	Tree	Pattai	Internal	Charu
Avarai	***Cassia auriculata***	Fabaceae	Tree	Poo	External	kattu
Iththi	***Ficusmicrocarpa***	Moraceae	Tree	Pinju, Pattai	Internal	Kudineer, Karkam
Ilavankappattai	***Cinnamomumverum***	Lauraceae	Tree	Pattai	Internal	Kudineer
Oothimaram	***Lanneacoromandelica***	Anacardiaceae	Tree	Pattai	External	Peechu
Kanja	***Cannabis sativa***	Cannabaceae	Shrub	Whole plant	Internal	Kudineer
Kadarpasi	***Gracilarialichenoides***	Gracilariaceae	Algae	Patchai	Internal	Karkam
Kattukodi	***Cocculushirsutus***	Menispermaceae	Creeper	Illai, Ver	Internal	Kudineer
Karunkalli	***Acacia catechu***	Fabaceae	Tree	Pisin	Internal	Kudineer
Kavizhthumbai	***Trichodesmaindicum***	Boraginaceae	Herb	Illai	Internal	Kudineer
Kasa	***Memecylonumbellatium***	Melastomataceae	Shrub	Ver	Internal	Kudineer
Kothumai	***Triticum aestivum***	Poaceae	Grass	Arisi	Internal	Utkalli
Sathikkai	***Myristicafragrans***	Myristicaceae	Tree	Kai	Internal	Chooranam
Sayamaram	***Caesalpiniasappan***	Fabaceae	Tree	Marachakkai	External	Peechu
Sirunagapoo	***Mesuanagassarium***	Calophyllaceae	Tree	Poo	Internal	Chooranam
Sembarathai	***Hibiscus rosa - sinensis***	Malvaceae	Shrub	Poo	Internal	Kudineer
Thippilli	***Piper longum***	Piperaceae	Climber	Kai, Arisi	Internal	Chooranam

(*Contd...*)

Thenku	***Cocos nucifera***	Arecaceae	Tree	ver	Internal	kudineer
Thetran	***Strychnospotatorum***	Loganiaceae	Tree	Whole plant	Internal	Kudineer
Naval	***Syzygiumcumini***	Myrtaceae	Tree	Pattai	Internal	Karkam
Nilapoosani	***Ipomeamauritiana***	Convolvulaceae	Creeper	Kizhanku	Internal	Legium
Nettilingam	***Polyalthialongifolia***	Anonaceae	Tree	Pattai	Internal	Kudineer
Neitharkizhanku	***Nymphaea pubescens***	Nymphaeaceae	Aquatic plant	Poo	Internal	Kudineer
Nel	***Oryza sativa***	Poaceae	Grass	Arisi	Internal	Pittu
Nelli	***Phyllanthus emblica***	Phyllanthaceae	Tree	Whole plant	Internal	Kudineer
Pannimonthankizhanku	***Trapanatans***	Lythraceae	Shrub	Vithai	Internal	Karkam
Sirupeelai	***Aervalanata***	Amaranthaceae	Herb	Verpattai	Internal	Karkam
Poonaikalli	***Mucunapruriens***	Fabaceae	Climber	Vithai	Internal	Legium
Mantharai	***Bauhinia purpurea***	Fabaceae	Tree	Poo	Internal	Kudineer
Maa	***Mangiferaindica***	Anacardiaceae	Tree	pisin	Internal	Kudineer
Masikkai	***Quercus infectoria***	Fagaceae	Tree	Kai	Internal	Chooranam
Mothakavalli	***Sterculiafoetida***	Malvaceae	Climber	Pattai	Internal	Kudineer
Valluluvai	***Celastruspaniculatus***	Celastraceae	Climber	Vithai	Internal	Chooranam
Vaazhai	***Musa paradisiaca***	Musaceae	Tree	Poo	Internal	Charu
Vila	***Limoniaacidissima***	Rutaceae	Tree	Pisin	Internal	Chooranam
Velliloththiram	***Symplocosracemosa***	Symplocaceae	Shrub	Pattai	Internal	Kudineer

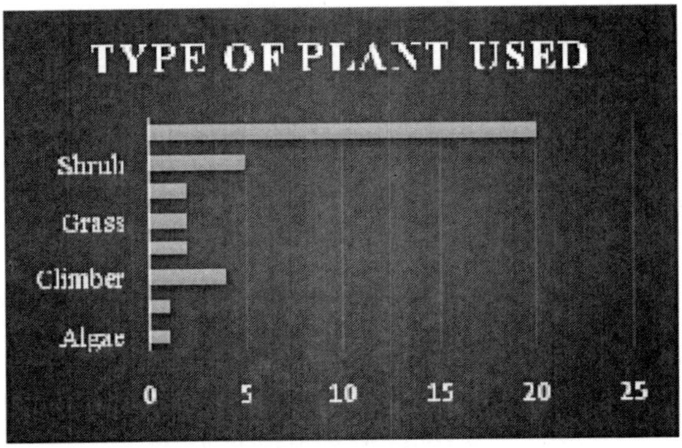

Fig no. 1.1: Type of plant used.

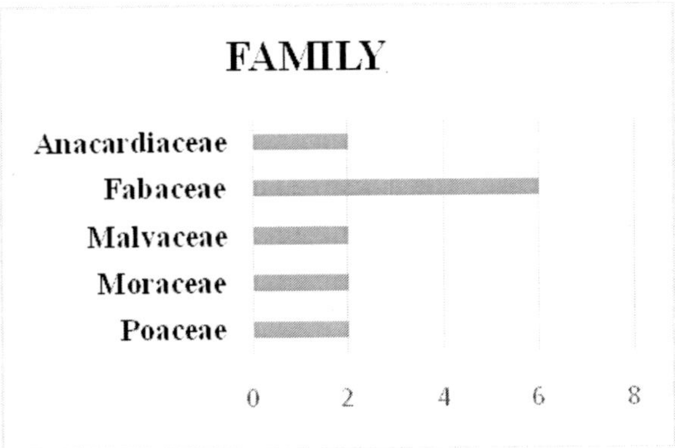

Fig no. 1.2: Halitat of plants.

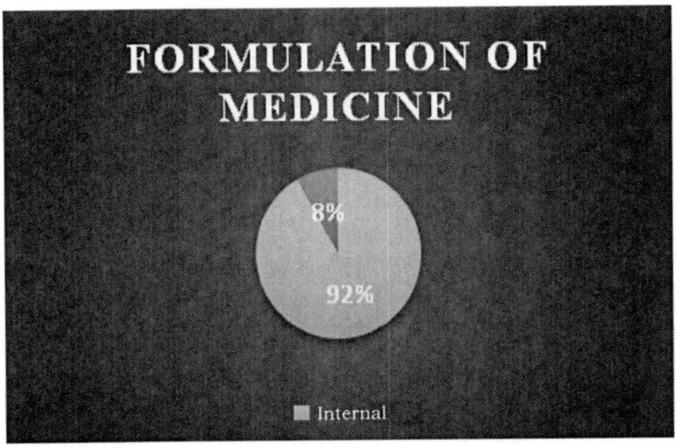

Fig no. 1.3: Formulation of medicine.

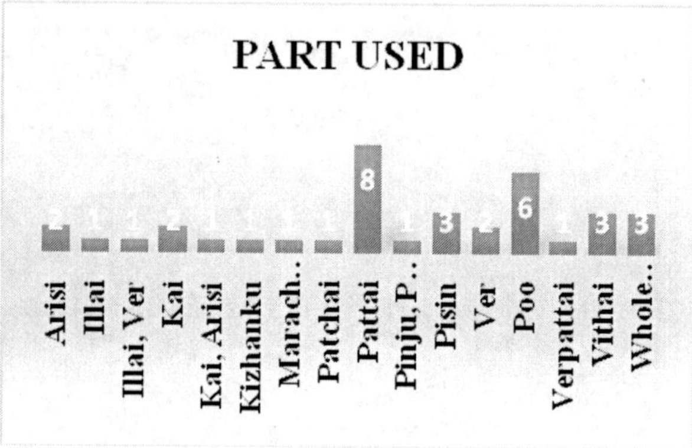

Fig no. 1.4: part of the plant used.

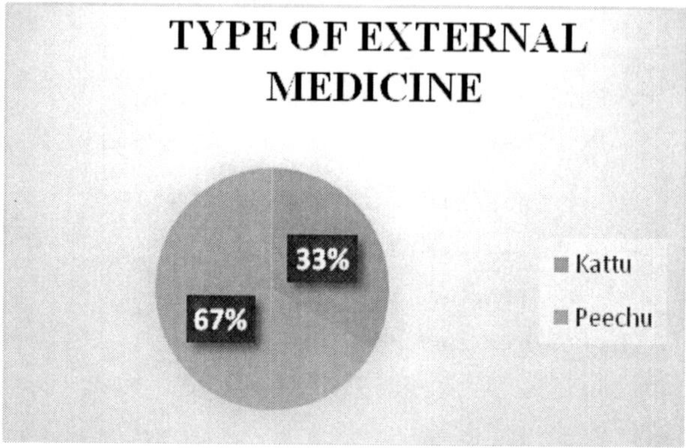

Fig no. 1.5: Type of external medicine.

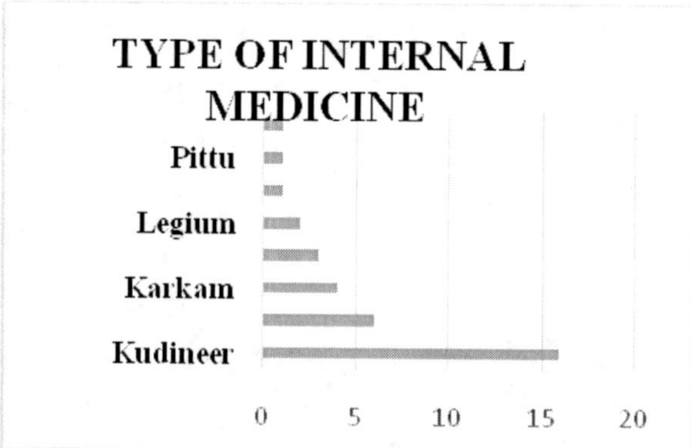

Fig no. 1.6: Type of internal medicine.

Dysmenorrhoea

Plant name	*Botanical name*	*Family*	*Type of plant*	*Use of plant*	*Type of medicine*	*Formulation of medicine*
Abini	***Papaver somniferum***	Papavaraceae	Herb	Paal	External	Thylam
Araththai	***Alpinia galanga***	Zingiberaceae	Shrub	Ver	External	Thylam
Etti	***Strychnosnux vomica***	Loganaceae	Tree	Verpattai	Internal	Kudineer
Kurosanioomam	***Hyoscyamusniger***	Solanaceae	Herb	Vithai	Internal	Kudineer
Kadalai	***Cicer arietinum***	Fabaceae	Climber	Whole plant	External	Vedhu
Kariyapolam	***Aloe littoralis***	Asphodelaceae	Herb	Paal	Internal	Mathirai
Kattukaduku	***Cleome viscosa***	Cleomaceae	Herb	Whole plant	External	Pattru
Malaivembu	***Melia azedarachta***	Meliaceae	Tree	Verpattai	Internal	Chooranam
Seemaimilakai	***Capsicum frutescens***	Solanaceae	Climber	Kai	Internal	Kudineer
Masipatchai	***Artemisia nilagirica***	Asteraceae	Herb	Illai	Internal	Charu
Perunkayam	***Ferula asafoetida***	Apiaceae	Shrub	Pisin	Internal	Melugu
Punnai	***Calophylluminophyllum***	Calophyllaceae	Tree	Kottai	Internal	Chooranam
Punku	***Pongamiapinnata***	Fabaceae	Tree	Vithai	External	Thylam
Pakal	***Momordica charantia***	Cucurbitaceae	Climber	Palam	Internal	Charu
Nelli	***Phyllanthus emblica***	Phyllanthaceae	Tree	Whole plant	Internal	Kudineer
Thetran	***Strychnospotatorum***	Loganaceae	Tree	Whole plant	Internal	Kudineer
Sathikkai	***Myristicafragrans***	Myristicaceae	Tree	Kai	Internal	Chooranam
Aaruvatha	***Rutachalepensis***	Rutaceae	Herb	Illai	Internal	Charu

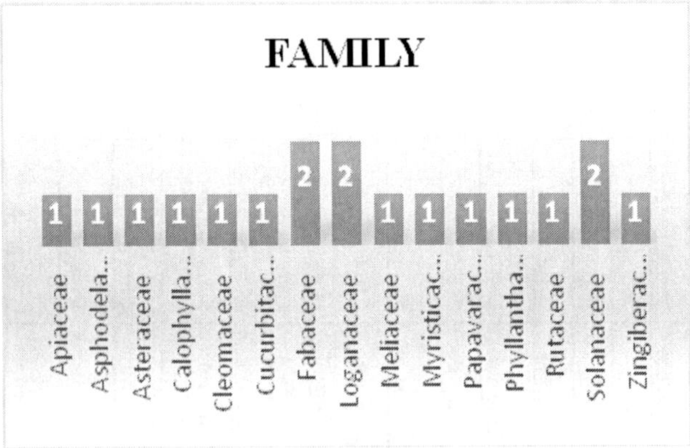

Fig no. 2.1: Family of the plants.

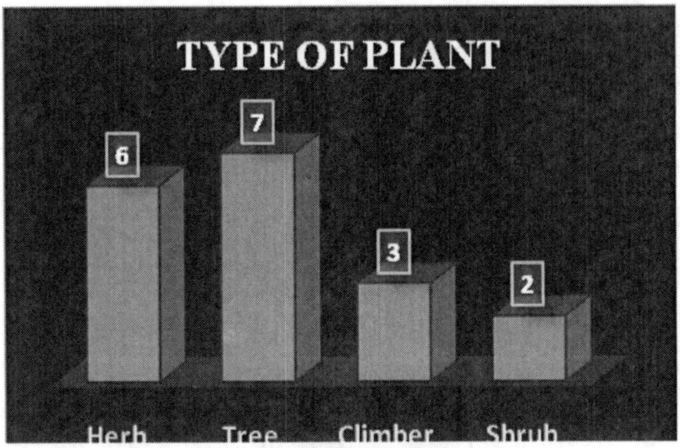

Fig no. 2.2: Type of the plants.

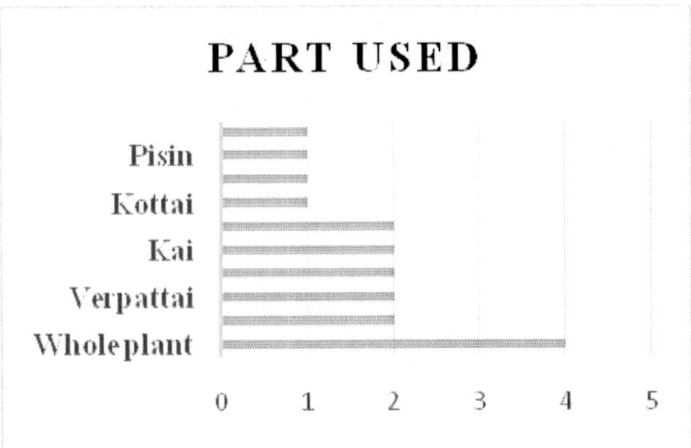

Fig no. 2.3: Part of plants used.

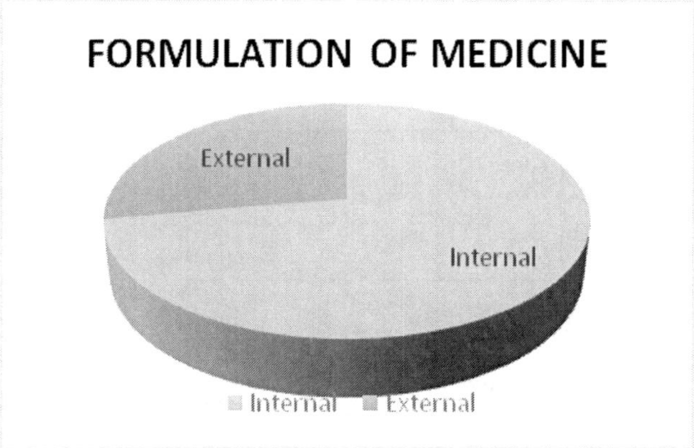

Fig no. 2.4: Type of medicine.

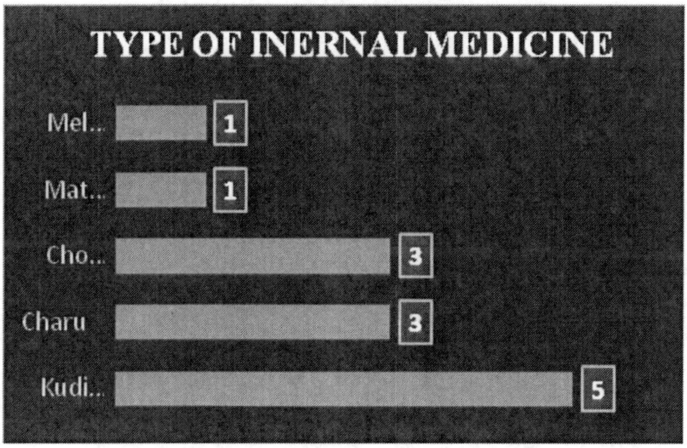

Fig no. 2.5: Type of internal medicine.

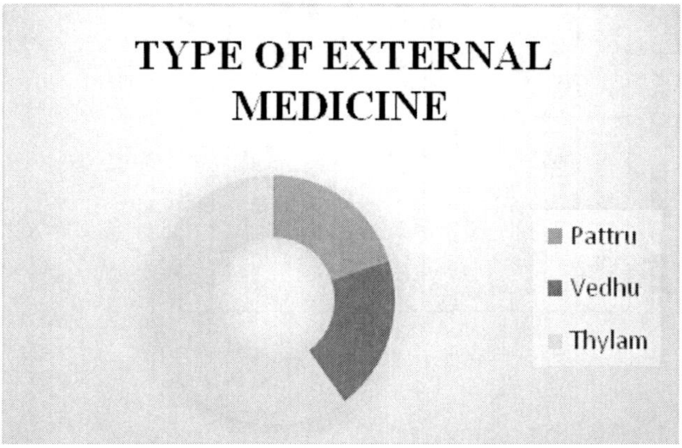

Fig no. 2.6: Type of external medicine.

Amenorrhoea

Plant name	*Botanical name*	*Family*	*Type of plant*	*Part used*	*Type of medicine*	*Formulation of medicine*
Annasipazham	***Ananuscomosus***	Bromeliaceae	Shrub	Pazham	Internal	Charu
Aalivirai	***Lepidium sativum***	Brassicaceae	Tree	Vithai	Internal	Kudineer
Illaththalari	***Plumeria rubra***	Apocyanaceae	Tree	Whole plant	External	Pattru
Ell	***Sesamum indicum***	Pedaliaceae	Herb	Vithai	Internal	Kudineer
Kariyapolam	***Aloe littoralis***	Asphodelaceae	Herb	Ver	Internal	Kudineer
Thalai	***Pandanus odoratissimus***	Pandanaceae	Shrub	Whole plant	Internal	Karkam
Nayuruvi	***Achyranthes aspera***	Amaranthaceae	Herb	Ver	Internal	Kudineer
Masippatchai	***Artemisia nilagirica***	Asteraceae	Herb	Ilai	Internal	Charu
Venkayam	***Allium cepa***	Amaryllidaceae	Herb	Kizhanku	Internal	Karkam
Vellilothiram	***Symplocosracemosa***	Symplocaceae	Tree	Pattai	Internal	Kudineer

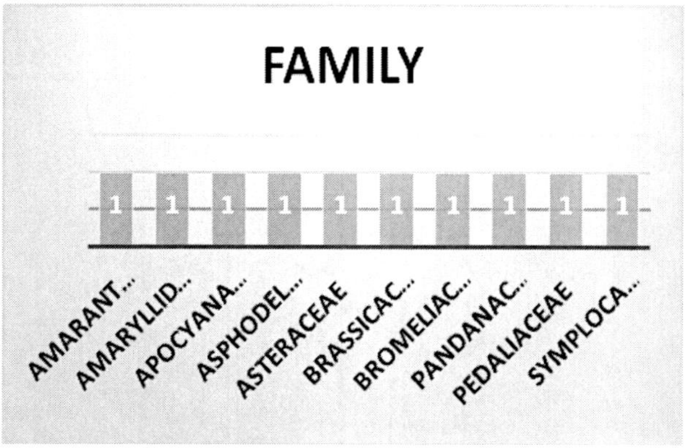

Fig no. 3.1: Family of the plants.

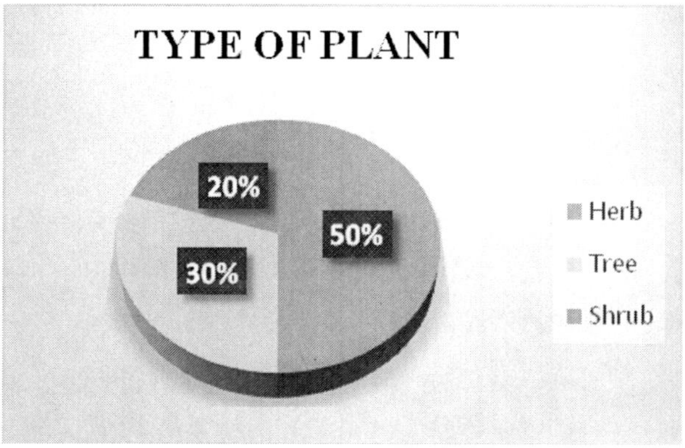

Fig no. 3.2: Type of halitat.

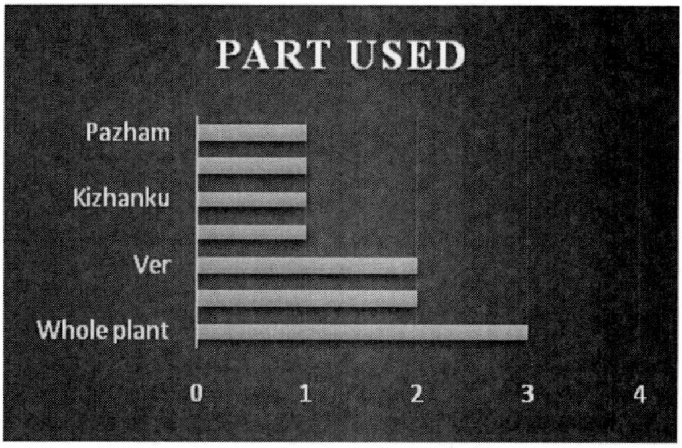

Fig no. 3.3: Part of plant used.

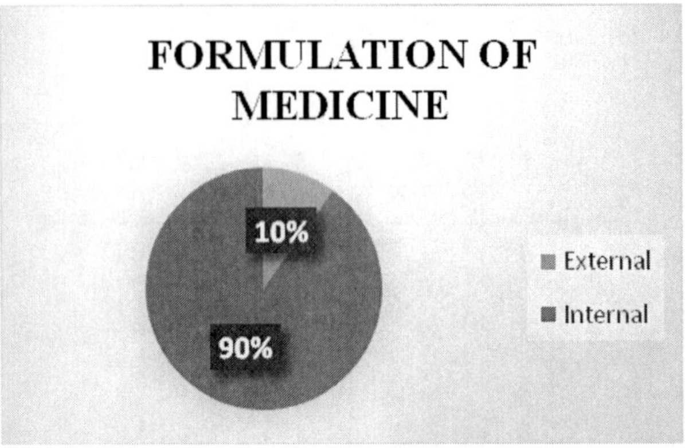

Fig no. 3.4: Type of medicine.

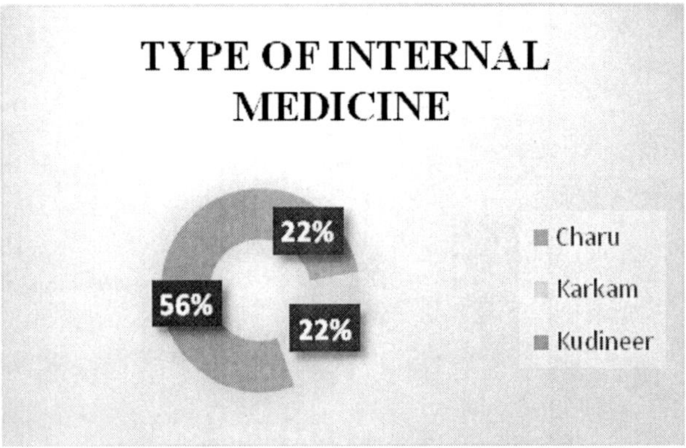

Fig no. 3.5: Type of internal medicine.

Discussion and Conclusion

Siddha system is very effective medicine in this world. In siddha medical text book reffered the "**Siddha materiamedica**" reveals siddha management for menstrual problems in women's life. In this research had a solution of major three menstrual problems that is menorrhagia, dysmenorrhoea and amenorrhoea. In this research about menorrhagia recorded as 37 raw materials. This raw materials occupied 28 families mainly occupied family is Fabaceae (06) and anacardiaceae, Malvaceae, Moraceae, Poaceae are occupied 02 times. 07 type of internal medicine and 02 type of external medicine were noted. In internal medicine Kudineer (16), Chooranam (6), Karkam (4), Charu (3), Legium (2) are mostly used. And then treatment of dysmenorrhoea recorded as 18 raw materials. This raw materials occupied 15 families; most occupied families are Fabaceae (2), Loganaceae (2), Solanaceae (2). This symptomatic treatment include 13 type of internal medicine and 05 type of external medicine. Internal medicine include Kudineeer (5), Charu (3), Chooranam(3), Mathirai (3), Melugu (1) and external medicine Thylam (13) are most time used. In amenorrhoea treatment 10 raw materials are recorded. This raw materials occupied 10 families. 09 type of internal medicine and 01 type of external medicine were noted this treatment and pattru used for external medicine for amenorrhoea.

Finally concluded as siddha medical system dealing with management of symptomatic treatment on menstrual problems (menorrhagia, dysmenorrhoea and amenorrhoea) in women's life at ancient time which management protocols should be established with proper scientific evidence based in future for man – kind purpose.

References

- Vaidya RathnamK. S. Murugesa Muthalitar, Edited by: Dr. Anaivaari R. Anandan, published by: Department of Indian Medicine & Homeopathy, Chennai 600 106, 1st edition - 1936, reprinted Year – 2013.
- American Academy of Pediatrics Committee on Adolescence: American College of Obstetricians and Gynecologists Committee on Adolescent Health Care: Diaz A, Laufer MR, Breech LL: Menstruation in girls and adolescents: using the menstrual cycle as a vital sign. Pediatrics 2006;118:2245-2250.
- Ibáñez L, Potau N, Zampolli M, et al: Hyperinsulinemia and decreased insulin-like growth factor-binding protein-1 are common features in prepubertal and pubertal girls with a history of premature pubarche. J Clin Endocrinol Metab1997;82:2283-2288.
- Deligeoroglou E, Tsimaris P, Deliveliotou A, et al: Menstrual disorders during adolescence. Pediatr Endocrinol Rev 2006;3:(suppl 1)150-159.

- The Practice Committee of the American Society for Reproductive Medicine: Current evaluation of amenorrhea. Fertil Steril 2008;90: (suppl 3) S219-S225.
- Patel SS, Bamigboye V: Hyperprolactinaemia. J Obstet Gynaecol 2007; 27: 455-459.
- Minjarez DA, Bradshaw KD: Abnormal uterine bleeding in adolescents. Obstet Gynecol Clin North Am 2000;27: 63-78.
- Biggs WS, Demuth RH. Premenstrual syndrome and premenstrual dysphoric disorder. Am Family Phys 2011; 84(8): 918- 924.
- Casablanca Y. Management of dysfunctional uterine bleeding. Obstet Gynecol Clin North Am 2008; 35(2):219- 234. Monawara et al 318 J Pharm Chem Biol Sci, June-August 2016; 4(2): 307-320.
- Laufer A, Breech MR. Menstruation in girls and adolescents: using the menstrual cycle as a vital sign. Pediatrics 2006; 118(5): 2245–2250.
- Silverthorn, Dee Unglaub. Human Physiology: An Integrated Approach. Glenview, IL: Pearson Education; 2013, p 850.
- Menstruation and the menstrual cycle fact sheet. USA: Office of Women's Health; 2014.
- Osayande AS, Mehulic S. Diagnosis and initial management of dysmenorrhea. Am Family Phys 2014; 89 (5): 341–346.
- Cho SH, Hwang EW. Acupuncture for primary dysmenorrhea: a systematic review. BJOG 2010; 117(5):509-521.
- Tucker ME. Levonorgestrel system eases effects of menorrhagia. Medscape Medical News. Jan 09, 2013. Available at http://www.medscape.com/viewarticle/777406. Accessed: Jan 14, 2013.
- Gupta J, Kai J, Middleton L, et al. Levonorgestrel intrauterine system versus medical therapy for menorrhagia. N Engl J Med. 2013 Jan 10. 368(2):128-37. [Medline].
- DeCherney A, Polan ML. Hysteroscopic management of intrauterine lesions and intractable uterine bleeding. Obstet Gynecol. 1983 Mar. 61(3):392-7.
- [Medline] Chen YJ, Li YT, Huang BS, Y, et al, for the Taiwan Association of Gynecology Systematic Review Group. Medical treatment for heavy menstrual bleeding. Taiwan J Obstet Gynecol. 2015 Oct. 54 (5):483-8. [Medline].
- Hallberg L, Nilsson L. Determination of menstrual blood loss. Scand J Clin Lab Invest. 1964. 16:244-8. [Medline].

10

Factors Influencing in Nutritional Status of Women in India

— *Dr. R. Nageswari*

Abstract

Women form a significant vulnerable segment of population that comprise around one-tenth of Indian population, Undernutrition among women is a genuine and general medical issue universally, particularly in developing nations. The stage of women after the primary year of life is the basic time for quick physical development and changes in body synthesis, physiology and endocrine. One of the major issues of India is undernutrition among children. The nation is yet battling with this issue. Malnutrition, arises because of flawed nutrition. It debilitates the invulnerable framework and causes huge damage and psychological deferral. Development appraisal is the estimation that best characterizes the health and nutritional status of children, while additionally gives a roundabout estimation of prosperity for the whole population. India, a developing nation covers 40% of undernourished offspring of the world. In India, ancestral population is among the most denied and undernourished individuals. Health and nutrition of the present women may have incredible effect on the nature of people to come. Appropriate nutritional status and health strategies should executed among the juvenile young girls to tackle the issue of undernutrition and comparable examinations ought to be arranged in other oppressed segments around the world.

Keywords: *Undernutrition, Malnutrition, Growth Assessment, Womens and Nutritional Status.*

Introduction

'The Ministry of Women and Child Development is fundamentally engaged with the issues of nutrition and advancement of children, especially women. The planned stations and booked clans have been distinguished as the two most distraught gatherings of Indian culture requiring unique consideration. Strengthening of the women is important, as it assist her adapt to the progressions and advance familiarity with health especially nutrition and conceptive health, in order to break the intergenerational life cycle of nutritional and sexual orientation inconvenience and give an empowering and supporting condition for self-improvement. Social welfare division, as for the financial status of Scheduled Caste population and socio scholastic profile of the booked position women, has been keeping up school goings as a star instructive measure. Women's health covers nutritional status, bleakness, and regenerative health. During the time of pre-adulthood, the supplement needs are the best. The young girls are normally physically hindered a sign of endless protein vitality malnutrition. An enormous extent of womens experiences the ill effects of different gynecological issues, especially menstrual abnormalities, for example, menorrhagia, polymenorrhea, oligomenorrhea, and dysmenorrhea. In India, the welfare Programs for women are taken care by the Education and Social welfare division. These establishments are keep running comparable to class goings and are being kept running in summer excursion too. To accomplish this goal, the Government of India has begun an enormous number of social welfare exercises for women. So, it is mandatory to study the factors influencing the nutritional status of women in India.

Research Objectives

The present study has been conducted with following objectives:

1. To know the status of women in India.

2. To highlight the factors influencing the nutritional status of women in India.
3. To give suggestions to overcome the malnutrition problem among women in India.

Operational Definitions

Nutrition is the science that deciphers the communication of supplements and different substances of nutrition in connection to upkeep, development, propagation, health and infection of a life form. It incorporates sustenance consumption, ingestion, osmosis, biosynthesis, catabolism, and discharge.

Nutritional status is a prerequisite strength of an individual persuaded by the eating regimen, the levels of supplements containing in the body and ordinary metabolic honesty. Typical nutritional status is overseen by parity sustenance utilization and ordinary use of supplements.

Reviews of Related Literatures

Pascual (1971) analysed the impact of social and social factors on sustenance propensities and reason for malnutrition. He talked about the significance of socio-social components like traditions, convictions, nutrition propensities and conventions that influence the nutritional status. As per his research, tragically mental, social and social elements, which make boundaries against the adjustment in sustenance propensities, are not seen appropriately, while numerous examinations just focussed on the unoriginal parts of nutrition and malnutrition.

A. Chandrasekar and D. Xaviour (1998) directed an investigation on the nutritional status of the Adi Karnataka people group who were observed to be of lower medium stature with a normal body fabricated. The investigation uncovered higher recurrence of females than guys in the age gatherings of 0-14 years and 65+ years, though in the age gatherings of 15-44 years and 45-64 years, the switch pattern was seen among the Adi Karnataka individuals, utilization of fat and calcium were observed to be higher.

Status of Womens in India

The status of women in India has been subject to many changes over the span of recorded Indian history. Their position in society deteriorated early in India's ancient period, especially in the Indo-Aryan speaking regions, and their subordination continued to be reified well into India's early modern period. Practises such as female infanticide, dowry, child marriage and the taboo on widow remarriage, have had a long duration in India, and have proved difficult to root out, especially in caste Hindu society in northern India. During the British East India Company rule (1757–1857), and the British Raj (1858–1947), measures aiming at amelioration were enacted, including Bengal Sati Regulation, 1829, Hindu Widows' Remarriage Act, 1856, Female Infanticide Prevention Act, 1870, and Age of Consent Act, 1891. Women's rights under the Constitution of India mainly include equality, dignity, and freedom from discrimination; additionally, India has various statutes governing the rights of women. As of 2018, some women have served in various senior official positions in the Indian government, including that of the President of India, the Prime Minister of India, the Speaker of the Lok Sabha. However, many women in India continue to face significant difficulties. The rates of malnutrition are exceptionally high among adolescent girls and pregnant and lactating women in India, with repercussions for children's health. Violence against women, especially sexual violence, has been on the rise in India.

Factors Influencing in Nutritional Status of Women

The components influencing nutritional equalization differ generally and influence the effectiveness of supplement use.

Natural determinants of Nutritional Level

Craving and satiety:

Our physiological needs give the fundamental determinants of nutritional level. People need vitality and supplements so as to endure and react to the sentiments of yearning and satiety (fulfilment of craving, condition of no appetite between two eating events). The focal sensory system is associated with controlling the harmony between craving, hunger incitement and sustenance consumption. The large scale supplements for example sugars, proteins and fats produce satiety sign of shifting quality. The parity of proof recommends that fat has the least satisfying force, starches have a halfway impact and protein has been observed to be the most satisfying. The vitality thickness of weight control plans has been appeared to apply intense impacts on satiety; low vitality thickness diets create more prominent satiety than high vitality thickness eats less carbs. The high vitality thickness of high-fat and additionally high-sugar nutrition can likewise prompt 'aloof overconsumption', where abundance vitality is ingested accidentally and without the utilization of extra mass. A significant satiety sign might be the volume of sustenance or segment size devoured. Numerous individuals are uninformed of what establishes proper bit sizes and in this way incidentally devour overabundance vitality.

Acceptability:

Acceptability is corresponding to the joy somebody encounters when eating a specific sustenance. It is subject to the tactile properties of the sustenance, for example, taste, smell, surface and appearance. Sweet and high-fat substances have a certain tactile intrigue. It isn't astonishing then that sustenance isn't exclusively viewed as a wellspring of sustenance yet is frequently expended for the delight esteem it grants. The impact of satisfactoriness on hunger and nutrition admission in people has been researched in a few examinations. There is an expansion in sustenance admission as agreeability increments, yet the impact of attractiveness on craving in the period following utilization is misty. Expanding sustenance assortment can likewise build nutrition and vitality admission and in the present moment modify vitality balance. Be that as it may, consequences for long haul vitality guideline are obscure.

Tangible viewpoints:

'Taste' is reliably announced as a noteworthy impact on sustenance conduct. As a general rule 'taste' is the whole of all tangible incitement that is created by the ingestion of sustenance. This incorporates taste fundamentally as well as smell, appearance and surface of sustenance. These tangible angles are thought to impact, specifically, unconstrained nutritional level. Since the beginning, taste and recognition impact conduct towards sustenance. A preference for sweetness and an aversion for sharpness are viewed as intrinsic human qualities, present from birth. Taste inclinations and nutrition revulsions create through encounters and are impacted by our frames of mind, convictions and desires.

Economic and Physical Determinants of Nutritional Level

Cost and openness:

There is no uncertainty that the expense of nutrition is an essential determinant of nutritional level. Regardless of whether cost is restrictive depends on a very basic level on an individual's salary and financial status. Low-pay gatherings have a more noteworthy propensity to devour lopsided weight control plans and specifically have low admissions of leafy foods. Be that as it may, access to more cash does not naturally compare to a superior quality eating routine but rather the scope of nutrition from which one can pick should increment. Availability to shops is another significant physical factor affecting nutritional level, which is subject to assets, for example, transport and geological area. Solid nutrition will in general be increasingly costly when accessible inside towns and urban communities contrasted with grocery stores on the outskirts19. In any case, improving access alone does not build buy of extra leafy foods, which are as yet viewed as restrictively costly.

Education and Knowledge:

Studies show that the level of education can impact dietary conduct during adulthood. Interestingly, nutrition learning and great dietary propensities are not firmly related. This is on the grounds that information about health does not prompt direct activity when people are uncertain how to apply their insight. Besides, data dispersed on nutrition originates from an assortment of sources and is seen as clashing or is doubted, which demoralizes inspiration to change. In this way, it is imperative to pass on exact and predictable messages through different media, on nutrition bundles and obviously by means of health experts.

Social determinants of Nutritional Level

Impact of social class:

What individuals eat is shaped and compelled by conditions that are basically social and social. Population studies appear there are clear contrasts in social classes as to nutrition and supplement admissions. Less than stellar eating routines can result in under-(micronutrients insufficiency) and over-nutrition (vitality over utilization bringing about overweight and corpulence); issues that face various areas of society, requiring various levels of aptitude and techniques for mediation.

Social impacts:

Social impacts lead to the distinction in the ongoing utilization of specific nutrition and in conventions of arrangement, and in specific cases can prompt confinements, for example, prohibition of meat and milk from the eating regimen. Social impacts are anyway managable to change: when moving to another nation people regularly embrace specific nutrition propensities for the nearby culture.

Social context:

Social effects on nutrition admission allude to the effect that at least one people have on the eating conduct of others, either immediate (purchasing sustenance) or backhanded (gain from companion's conduct), either cognizant (move of convictions) or subliminal. Notwithstanding when eating alone, nutritional level is impacted by social variables since dispositions and propensities create through the connection with others. In any case, evaluating the social effects on nutrition admission is troublesome in light of the fact that the impacts that individuals have on the eating conduct of others are not constrained to one sort and individuals are not really mindful of the social impacts that are applied on their eating conduct. Social help can beneficially affect nutritional levels and refreshing dietary change. Social help from inside the family unit and from colleagues was emphatically connected with upgrades in leafy foods utilization and with the preparative phase of improving dietary patterns, separately. Social help may upgrade health advancement through cultivating a feeling of gathering having a place and helping individuals to be increasingly able and self-solid. The family is generally perceived as being noteworthy in nutrition choices. Research demonstrates the forming of nutritional levels occurring in the home. Since family and companions can be a wellspring of consolation in making and continuing dietary change, receiving dietary methodologies which are adequate to them may profit the individual while likewise affecting the dietary patterns of others.

Social setting:

Despite the fact that most of sustenance is eaten in the home, an expanding extent is eaten outside the home, for example in schools, at work and in eateries. The scene wherein sustenance is eaten can influence nutritional level, especially as far as what nutrition are on offer. The accessibility of solid sustenance at home and 'far from home' expands the utilization of such nutrition. In any case, access to sound sustenance choices is constrained in many work/ school situations. This is especially valid for those with unpredictable hours or with specific prerequisites, for example veggie lover. With most of grown-up girls and men in business, the impact of work on health practices, for example, nutritional levels is a significant region of examination.

Meal Patterns

Individuals have a wide range of eating events day by day, the inspirations for which will vary starting with one event then onto the next. Most examinations explore the components that impact routine nutritional level yet it might be helpful to research what impacts nutritional level at various eating events. The impacts of eating on health have been discussed broadly. Proof demonstrates that nibbling can have impacts on vitality and supplement admissions however not really on weight index. Be that as it may, ordinary weight and overweight people may contrast in their adapting procedures when nibble nutrition are unreservedly accessible and furthermore in their compensatory instruments at ensuing dinners. In addition, nibble arrangement might be a significant viewpoint in the capacity of people to change admission to address vitality issues. Helping women grown-ups to pick sound nibble decisions represents a test to numerous health experts. In the home, instead of prohibiting undesirable bites, a progressively positive methodology might be the presentation of solid nibble alternatives after some time. In addition, solid nutritional levels outside the home likewise should be made all the more promptly accessible.

Physical variables

Stress:

Mental pressure is a typical element of current life and can adjust practices that influence health, for example, physical action, smoking or nutritional level. The impact of weight on nutritional level is perplexing not least due to the different sorts of pressure one can understanding. The impact of weight on sustenance admission relies upon the individual, the stressor and the conditions. All in all, a few people eat more and some eat not exactly typical when encountering pressure. The proposed systems for stress instigated changes in eating and nutritional level are persuasive contrasts (decreased worry about weight control), physiological (diminished craving brought about by the procedures related with pressure) and down to earth changes in eating openings, sustenance accessibility and feast arrangement. Concentrates likewise propose that in the event that work pressure is delayed or visit, at that point antagonistic dietary changes could result, expanding the likelihood of weight gain and thusly cardiovascular hazard.

Mind-set:

Hippocrates was the first to propose the mending intensity of sustenance, notwithstanding, it was not until the medieval times that nutrition was viewed as an instrument to adjust demeanor and temperament. Today it is perceived that sustenance impacts our disposition and that mind-set has a solid impact over our decision of nutrition. Curiously, it creates the impression that the impact of sustenance on temperament is connected to a limited extent to frames of mind towards specific nutrition. The irresolute association with sustenance – needing to appreciate it yet aware of weight increase is a battle experienced by many. Health food nuts, individuals with high restriction and a few girls report feeling regretful on account of not eating what they figure they should. Also, endeavours to limit admission of specific nutrition can expand the longing for these specific sustenance, prompting what are portrayed as nutrition yearnings. Girls more ordinarily report nutrition yearnings than do men. Discouraged temperament seems to impact the seriousness of these yearnings. Reports of nutrition desires are likewise progressively basic in the premenstrual stage, when complete sustenance admission increments and a parallel change in basal metabolic rate happen. In this way, mind-set and stress can impact nutritional level conduct and potentially short and long haul reactions to dietary mediation.

Dietary issues:

Eating conduct, not at all like numerous other organic capacities, is regularly subject to complex intellectual control. A standout amongst the most broadly polished types of intellectual command over nutrition admission is consuming less calories. Numerous people express a craving to get in shape or improve their body shape and consequently take part in ways to deal with accomplish their optimal weight file. Be that as it may, issues can emerge when abstaining from excessive food intake as well as exercise are taken to limits. The etiology of dietary issues is normally a mix of variables including natural, mental, familial and socio-social. The event of dietary issues is frequently connected with a contorted mental self view, low confidence, non-explicit tension, fixation, stress and despondency. Treatment of a dietary problem by and large requires weight adjustment and coordinated psychotherapy.

Aversion is increasingly hard to characterize however recommendations incorporate shirking of tyke misuse; evasion of amplifying diet and medical problems; appearing without over-controlling; not setting unimaginable norms; compensating little achievements in the present; empowering freedom and friendliness.

Suggestions to Overcome the Malnutrition Problem Among Women in India

Plainly the issue of malnutrition in India is of disturbing size, yet additionally of incredible multifaceted nature. A noteworthy piece of this issue is contributed by ghetto population. Handling malnutrition in India requires an all encompassing methodology. For successful usage of this methodology in urban ghettos following intercessions are suggested.

1. Aptitudes based nutrition education for the family

Nutrition education should address family in general and not simply the girls. Nutrition education should concentrate on correspondence for social change. The nutrition-related exercises should be founded on subjective research that has recognized social and institutional limitations to great nutrition, adverse frames of mind and practices toward sustenance and eating conduct. With imaginative reasoning, nutrition and health related exercises can be joined into gathering exercises, however should be seen to be significant to their ways of life as opposed to forced.

2. Stronghold of nutrition things

Any sustenance ware, be it sugar, milk, heartbeats, rice or sauces can be sustained with micronutrients.

3. Powerful disease control

In school conditions, women are particularly defenceless to a large group of diseases that bargain their health and invulnerability and, thus, their nutritional status.

Malnutrition and women sicknesses are interconnected and commonly strengthen each other. It is along these lines critical that women ailments are recognized, and fittingly treated, to contain the impact of the ailment on children health.

4. Preparing open social healthcare workers

Specialist organizations ought to be furnished with information and aptitudes to execute a nutrition program productively. Fitting preparing procedures and apparatuses should be created to prepare the specialist organizations. Prepared people group interface laborers don't just improve access to social insurance for the whole network yet additionally convey human services administrations and education to moms and children where the open medicinal services framework is missing.

5. Convey incorporated projects

Inter-sectoral cooperation is perceived as one of the methodologies to address issues of malnutrition. Nutrition education can have a huge impact in advancing good dieting propensities, and schools can add to decrease nutrition-related issues by incorporating nutrition mediations into an extensive health program.

Conclusion

Undernutrition was the key discoveries of the present investigation. Subsequently accentuation on primordial and essential preventive estimates like health education ought to be given for this segment of understudies. In this regard guardians as well as teachers ought to be prepared enough. Nutrition education might be made as a piece of school educational program separated from ordinary education exercises. Ordinary health and nutritional evaluation of the elementary younger students for early location and treatment is to be focused on more and current school health administrations projects ought to be additionally fortified. Mindfulness on neighbourhood creation of sound and sterile crisp nutrition is required. Better seepage offices, day by day trash freedom are should have been done under the periodical supervision.

References

- Arbyn, M.; Castellsague, X.; de Sanjose, S.; Bruni, L.; Saraiya, M.; Bray, F.; Ferlay, J. (6 April 2011). "Worldwide burden of cervical cancer in 2008". Annals of Oncology. 22 (12): 2675–2686.
- Carnes, Molly; Morrissey, Claudia; Geller, Stacie E. (November 2008). "Women's Health and Women's Leadership in Academic Medicine: Hitting the Same Glass Ceiling?". Journal of Women's Health. 17 (9): 1453–1462.
- Charney, Pamela (August 2000). "Women's health: An Evolving Mosaic". Journal of General Internal Medicine. 15 (8): 600–602.
- Charney, Pamela (4 December 2001). "Coronary Artery Disease in Young Women: The Menstrual Cycle and Other Risk Factors". Annals of Internal Medicine. 135 (11): 1002–1004.
- Clancy, Carolyn M.; Massion, Charlea T. (14 October 1992). "American Women's Health Care. A Patchwork Quilt with Gaps". JAMA. 268 (14): 1918–1920.
- Coney, Sandra; Bunkle, Phillida (June 1987). "An Unfortunate Experiment at National Women's" (PDF). Metro. Auckland. pp. 47–65. Retrieved 23 August 2016.
- Ellsberg, M. (September 2006). "Violence against women and the Millennium Development Goals: Facilitating women's access to support". International Journal of Gynecology & Obstetrics. 94 (3): 325–332. CiteSeerX 10.1.1.619.5166.
- Gahagan, Jacqueline; Gray, Kimberly; Whynacht, Ardath (2015). "Sex and gender matter in health research: addressing health inequities in health research reporting". International Journal for Equity in Health. 14 (1): 12.
- Gahagan, Jacqueline (15 August 2016). "Commentary on the new sex and gender editorial policy of the Canadian Journal of Public Health". Canadian Journal of Public Health. 107 (2): e140–1.
- García-Moreno, Claudia; Amin, Avni (1 May 2016). "The sustainable development goals, violence and women's and children's health". Bulletin of the World Health Organization. 94 (5): 396–397.
- Geller, Stacie E.; Adams, Marci Goldstein; Carnes, Molly (December 2006). "Adherence to Federal Guidelines for Reporting of Sex and Race/Ethnicity in Clinical Trials". Journal of Women's Health. 15 (10): 1123–1131.
- Geller, Stacie E.; Koch, Abby; Pellettieri, Beth; Carnes, Molly (March 2011). "Inclusion, Analysis, and Reporting of Sex and Race/

Ethnicity in Clinical Trials: Have We Made Progress?". Journal of Women's Health. 20 (3): 315–320.

- Gronowski, Ann M.; Schindler, Emily I. (2014). "Women's Health". Scand J Clin Lab Invest Suppl. 244: 2–7.
- Inhorn, Marcia C. (September 2006). "Defining Women's Health: A Dozen Messages from More than 150 Ethnographies" (PDF). Medical Anthropology Quarterly. 20 (3): 345–378.
- Kim, Esther S.H.; Carrigan, Thomas P.; Menon, Venu (August 2008). "Enrollment of Women in National Heart, Lung, and Blood Institute-Funded Cardiovascular Randomized Controlled Trials Fails to Meet Current Federal Mandates for Inclusion". Journal of the American College of Cardiology. 52 (8): 672–673.
- Koplan, Jeffrey P; Bond, T Christopher; Merson, Michael H; Reddy, K Srinath; Rodriguez, Mario Henry; Sewankambo, Nelson K; Wasserheit, Judith N (June 2009). "Towards a common definition of global health". The Lancet. 373 (9679): 1993–1995. CiteSeerX 10.1.1.610.7968.
- Liu, Katherine A.; DiPietro Mager, Natalie A. (31 March 2016). "Women's involvement in clinical trials: historical perspective and future implications". Pharmacy Practice. 14 (1): 708.
- McCarthy, CR (1994). "Historical background of clinical trials involving women and minorities". Acad Med. 69 (9): 695–698.
- Macfarlane, Sarah B; Jacobs, Marian; Kaaya, Ephata E (10 December 2008). "In the Name of Global Health: Trends in Academic Institutions". Journal of Public Health Policy. 29 (4): 383–401. doi:10.1057/jphp.2008.25. PMID 19079297.
- Marshall, N. L.; Tracy, A. J. (2009). "After the Baby: Work-Family Conflict and Working Mothers' Psychological Health". Family Relations. 58 (4): 380–391. doi:10.1111/j.1741-3729. 2009. 00560.x.
- Marshall, Nancy L. Employment and women's health. pp. 46–63. Retrieved 13 July 2016., in Spiers et al (2013).

11

A Study on Attitude towards Community Service of Women with Visual Impairment Doing Higher Education in Southern States

— *Dr. Kalpana. V*

Introduction

The women with visual impairment community are one of the most fragile communities in the society who needs enhancement and empowerment on their own. So every woman with visual impairment should represent for themselves in their community and also for other women like them in the society. For this community service attitude is a quintessential part for them which need to be inculcated as soon as possible. The researcher through this research has measured the community service attitude of women with visual impairment and also aimed at bringing out the success of many women with visual impairment in the southern states who are all the recipients of a scholarship named "Marga Schulze Scholarship Scheme for women with visual impairment doing higher education". It is a German based scholarship scheme which provides financial support to the meritorious girls with visual impairment in Asia and Africa to pursue their higher education.

An introduction about Community Service

The term community is used widely in our day to day language and in almost all walks of life. Various sectors like professionals, corporate and politicians use this term for different purposes. People in community live together for the achievement of common interests and common objectives. The responsible and active citizens are all well aware about the multiple needs of the community and have moral obligation to help the unprivileged sections. The participation of each member of the community is necessary to make the earth a better place to live in where all can share the available resources without any discrimination. This feeling of selfless service or service above self-interests for common good is community service **(Smith, 1994).** When some individuals or groups carry out such activities, which are beneficial for the masses, it is regarded as community service.

In the present context, community service means the service that an individual provides for the betterment of his or her locality or community, outside his family environment and does his best to fulfill the commitments towards the welfare of the society and the nation **(Clary and Orenstein, 1991).**

Nature of Community Service and Role of Education

Life is filled with opportunities. There are a number of ways through which a community member can serve those who are less fortunate. We can help others by doing physical, intellectual, spiritual and other kinds of services. Physical services encompass all those activities, which are performed to help others to meet their primary needs like food, clothing, shelter and safety. People also have intellectual needs. There are many people who fulfill the intellectual needs of the society. Teachers, professors, writers and journalists come in this category. The belief that education should produce a complete citizen, who is prepared to be an active member in the workforce and community, has long been the goal of education **(Sarkees – Wircenski and Scott, 2003)**.

Community Service learning holds great promises for higher education classrooms, it has generally been recognized that research into its outcomes and effects of service learning is lacking **(Eyler, Giles and Braxton, 1997; Giles, Honnet and Migliore, 1991)**.

There are five sub dimensions for community service attitude in this scale such as Awareness about Community Service, Commitment towards Community Service, Cost for Community Service, Benefits of Community Service and Myths about Community Service.

Review of Literature

An Overview

The review of literature plays a vital role in every research where it enables the researcher to get an insight about the research planned to do by knowing the studies done by the same area by other eminent persons such as academicians and professionals in the field. Few important literature reviews which inspired the researcher for the present study and the reviews which helped the research to expand and enhance the study are given in this part of the paper.

A review of available literature as related to the subject is an important and integral part of any research project. A critical survey of the literature on the subject will help in knowing the aims and objectives, methodology and findings of the previous studies done in the past. It could serve as a means of exchanging information and also helps to prevent further duplication of similar research. A review of literature thus helps in identifying the research gaps of a subject and need for the present study.

Reviews related to the study

Akankshi Singh Dr. R.P. Gupta in **February 2016** has published a research paper in IOSR Journal of Dental and Medical Sciences (IOSR-JDMS) titled "A research paper on the Employees Attitude towards organizational Change". This study has revealed that the most baffling and recalcitrant of the problems which business executives face is employee resistance to change. Resistance is usually created because of certain blind spots and employee attitudes with the technical aspects of new ideas. Management can take concrete steps to deal constructively with these employee attitudes. The steps include emphasizing new standards of performance and encouraging them to think in different ways, as well as making use of the fact that signs of resistance can serve as a practical warning signal in directing and timing technological changes. An organization must develop a new vision and a new faith in the workforce before it can approach the organizational change process. Managers must exhibit a trust in the workers to contribute to solving organizational problems, which in turn will build trust in management. The door must always be open for individuals to take an active role in improving the organization, allowing for open communication, initiative, and teamwork in problem solving.

As how the attitude of an employee plays a major role in an organization; likewise, the attitude of the women with VI beneficiaries of this scheme is also an important factor to be analyzed as they are going to be the future pioneers and role models for their community.

Lilian. K.Y. Li in **2012** has published a paper on "A study of the attitude, self-efficacy, effort and academic achievement of City students towards research methods and statistics" in Discovery – SS Student E-Journal Vol. In this study the relationship between social science students' attitude towards research methods and statistics, self-efficacy, effort and academic achievement. Self-administered questionnaire was chosen as the primary data collection method and a sample of 153 students from Department of Applied Social Studies in the City University of Hong Kong were invited to complete the survey. After analyzing the data collected, Pearson's correlation coefficient reflected that there was a positive correlation between all the four variables – attitude towards research methods and statistics, self-efficacy, effort and academic achievement. Also, a multiple regression analysis was conducted to estimate the prediction power of attitude and self-efficacy on effort. The result showed that both attitude and self-efficacy could significantly predict effort. However, when another multiple regression analysis was conducted to estimate the prediction power of attitude, self-efficacy and effort on academic achievement, it was found that effort failed to predict academic achievement. To conclude, in that study, effort could only be regarded as an indirect factor but not a necessary factor in bridging the relationship between attitude, self-efficacy and academic achievement.

This study has chosen the correlates to be an interlinked one and also relevant for the study, only after reading this paper the present study took community service attitude as one of the dimension for the study under the variable attitude.

Lauren Bradshaw in **October 2011** has written about a research paper titled "Research paper on Worker Attitude and Job Satisfaction" in an *online research paper writing service customwritings.com. In this the author has insisted that* a worker attitude towards work is directly linked to the job satisfaction; a worker who is satisfied with his job performs better and excels at what he does. It is therefore imperative for a company to understand the attitude of its workers and measure the job satisfaction of its employees, as job satisfaction is essential for productivity. The duty of management and the employee in improving worker's attitude is debatable. Some may argue that it is up to the employee to ensure that they attain job satisfaction from their work, as they are the only ones in control of their attitude and performance. It is also possible to say that all the responsibility is entirely the management's. They decide on the nature of the environment in which the employee works. The management holds the power to control employee salary, off time and promotion. External factors such as the environment, social situations, and culture also affect worker attitude and job satisfaction.

Likewise, the satisfaction of the scholarship beneficiaries lies on their good attitude. So, the researcher got an idea of assessing their attitude towards community service as an opinion arises that only the scholarship candidates who fully utilized the scholarship and excelled in their studies will only have the attitude to serve their community in return, as they will be in good career positions in their future.

The researcher wants to test this with all the beneficiaries, so that the result can either demystify the same or prove the same.

Research Methodology

Research is an art of scientific investigation and in common parlance refers to a search for knowledge. It is a scientific and systematic search for pertinent information on a specific research problem. Research methodology is a way to systematically solve the research problem. It outlines the entire research plan.

Statement of the research problem

Higher education forms the foundation for progression of Women with disabilities, as it ensures right to information, enriches them to communicate with others, and enhance them to assert their rights. So education plays a pivotal role in the lives of women with disabilities, that too for women with visual impairment.

In this research, the researcher covers the aspects such as, Social Economic and Environmental Conditions and Attitude towards Community Service of the women with visual impairment doing higher education in southern states.

Aim

The main aim of this research is to measure the attitude towards community service of women with visual impairment doing higher education in the southern states.

Objectives of the study

- To study the demographic profile of the beneficiaries of the scholarship scheme.
- To measure the attitude of the beneficiaries towards community service.
- To bring out the relationship between the demographic profile and attitude towards community service.
- **Research Design**

  The researcher adopted descriptive research design for this study as the study is descriptive and analytical.

Sampling

The researcher adopted Stratified random sampling method for the study in which disproportionate stratification was used.

Tools for Data Collection

The researcher adopted structured Questionnaire method to collect the data. The questionnaire consists of two parts in which the first part of the Questionnaire is the personal profile of the respondents. The second part consists of Community Service Attitude Scale (CSAS) designed by Rekha Rani and Punita Govil, 2016 which was used to measure the level of attitude towards community service of the respondents. The Reliability Coefficient for the study, Alpha Cronbach Coefficient was found to be 0.76.

Sources of Data Collection

The researcher used both primary and secondary sources for data collection. The primary data were collected with the help of Questionnaire by collecting the responses over phone (since they are women with visual impairment) and the questionnaire was mailed to respondents who had computer access. The researcher collected the data in different phases according to the convenience of the respondents. A significant amount of secondary data was collected from various sources such as books, journals, articles, magazines, reports, published data and e-materials and also from the scholarship implementing organizations CBM, Bangalore and UDIS Forum, Coimbatore.

Data Analysis

The collected data was coded and edited and was analyzed using SPSS.

Simple percentage, Mean and Standard Deviation was calculated which enabled to see the distribution of the respondents on their personal data and on the level of Community Service Attitude of women with visual impairment doing higher education.

Significant F test was applied to see whether two variances are equal. Here it is applied within two groups and between groups of personal variables and independent variable.

ANOVA was applied to find out the significant difference between the means of more than two groups of age, educational qualification, religion, place of dwelling, family type, family monthly income, marital status and occupational status with Community Service Attitude of the beneficiaries of the scholarship who are women with visual impairment.

Correlation was applied to find out the relationship between the personal variables and attitude towards community service attitude.

Factor analysis was done to find out the adequacy of sampling measure.

Findings of the Study

The researcher has made an attempt to find out the Socio economic and environmental conditions and Level of Community service attitude of the women with visual impairment doing higher education in southern states. The summary of the findings is given below.

Personal Profile of the women with visual impairment

Personal profile helps to understand the socio economic background of the women with visual impairment. The results of the study reveal that less than half of the respondents were in the younger age group of 21-25 years old and the rest of them were near to the middle age and above. More than half of the respondents have completed their UG degree and the rest of them have completed PG and B.Ed. degrees. A vast majority of the women with visual impairment who are beneficiaries of the scholarship are Hindus and it is also found that the meager rest of them are Christians and Muslims. More than half of the scholarship beneficiaries hail from urban areas while the other half are from rural areas. A good majority of them are from Nuclear families and the rest of them are from Joint families. Nearly half of the respondents' family monthly income ranges between Rs.10001 -15,000 and one third of them are in between the range 15001 – 20000. And the rest of them are within the ranges 20000 and above and there is very meager of them in the range 5000 and below. A good majority of the respondents are married and the rest of them are unmarried. A vast majority of the respondents are employed and the remaining of them are unemployed.

Findings related to the level of Community Service Attitude

Community Service Attitude

The results show that more than half of the respondents show neutral attitude towards community service and in the remaining only twenty-four percent has positive attitude and meager percent of them has negative attitude towards community service. Having neutral attitude is to an extent commendable but the women with visual impairment need to increase their attitude in serving their own community which was the objective of the scholarship scheme. The researcher felt that if intervention is done at the right time there is a chance for them to increase their attitude towards community service which the researcher meant here is doing service to their own community and not to community in general.

Finding related to Correlation between Community Service Attitude and demographic variables

To find out the relationship between the Community service attitude and the demographic variables among beneficiaries of the scholarship, Karl Pearson's Correlation test was applied.

Age and Community Service Attitude

The Karl Pearson's Correlation was applied to find out the relationship between the age and community service attitude and the result reveal that there is a negative correlation between the two variables. It means when the first variable increases the second variable decreases. So, it is clearly reported in this study that when Age increases the Community service attitude decreases.

Family Monthly income and Community Service Attitude

The Karl Pearson's Correlation was applied to find out the relationship between the family monthly income and community service attitude and the result reveal that there is a positive correlation between the two variables and thus when family monthly income increases the community service attitude also increases. Also as vice versa when family monthly income decreases the community service attitude also decreases.

Findings related to ANOVA (F test) and Independent Samples T test

Educational Qualification

To examine the difference between the means of groups based on educational qualification and community service attitude, ANOVA test was applied. The findings show that there is a difference in community service attitude between the groups with regard to educational qualification of the respondents. The Under graduation candidates and Post-graduation candidates differ less when compared to the B.Ed. candidates among the respondents who are women with visual impairment. The findings also reveal that the under graduation candidates have better attitude towards community service. As they have less educational burden than the other two groups may be their attitude towards community service is better when compared to the other two groups.

Religion

The ANOVA and F test results between the community service attitude and religion of the respondents reveal that they differ in their community service attitude with respect to religion.

Dwelling Place

The independent samples t test results reveal that there are differences in the means of the rural and urban groups of the respondents and the urban girls have better attitude towards community service than rural girls. This may be due to the lack of exposure for the rural girls.

Family Type

The independent samples t test results reveal that there are differences in the means of the nuclear family group and the joint family group of the respondents and hence they differ in community service attitude with respect to family type.

Marital Status

The independent samples t test results reveal that there are differences in the means of the married group and the unmarried group of the respondents and hence they do not differ in community service attitude with respect to marital status. Both married and unmarried cases have better community service attitude.

Occupational status

The independent samples t test results reveal that there are differences in the means of the employed and unemployed groups of the respondents. The employed group has better community service attitude.

Findings related to Factor analysis on Community Service attitude

Kaiser-Meyer-Olkin (KMO) test and Bartlett's test

The factor analysis done on the community service attitude reveal that the Kaiser-Meyer-Olkin (KMO) test and Bartlett's test result to measure the sampling measure reveal that the sampling is adequate.

Conclusion

The status of women in the society is always an invincible one and is a road to development and success in any country. It is always an arguable debate whether women should take up all lead roles in the country and to head a flourishing field in a country. The current status of the beneficiaries of the scholarship is definitely astounding to know and those were the real success of the Marga Schulze Scholarship Scheme too. But this is not enough for the entire women with visual impairment community and they have to be enhanced and empowered as a community and not only as individuals to forego changes at larger level and to lead a standard living besides their disability. The researcher really wanted to bring a clear insight about the aspects of the women with visual impairment doing higher education in southern states and their attitude towards community service and also their social, economic and environmental conditions.

In this study the Social, Economic and environmental conditions and Community service attitude of the women with visual impairment doing higher education was studied. The study included a sample of 234 scholarship beneficiaries who are women with visual impairment located in the southern states of India. The data were collected using a structured questionnaire. The data were analyzed using SPSS software. The findings of the study revealed that the scholarship beneficiaries who are women with visual impairment were having neutral attitude towards community service. The findings also revealed that there was a significant difference found between the personal variables and study variable. Further correlation results showed a significant relationship among personal variables and attitude towards community service of women with visual impairment doing higher education in southern states.

12

Health Care Access Barriers of Sri Lankan Tamil Camp Living Refugees in Tamil Nadu

— ***Maneesh P, Dr. C. Muniyandi***

Abstract

Health is a fundamental human right and is also considered as a worldwide social goal. It is an important determinant of well being and health care is regarded as a public right, and important responsibility governments to provide this care to all people irrespective of race, religion, caste or creed, rural or urban, rich or poor. In India, the effort to improve the health status of the population is a major thrust and it is under the social development programme being undertaken in India. Public health programmes play a very significant role in the physical and mental well being of every nation. The improvement of the health status of people is connected to several factors such as household income, public expenditure on healthcare delivery system, availability of private healthcare facilities and general environmental conditions affecting the incidence of diseases. The health status of the population of a nation was assumed to affect the utility of the people directly by the value that individuals place on good health and indirectly through increasing healthy time and labour income of the person. Unlike the health service avail to the citizens, the same made available to refugees who are living in the country. This study attempted to analyse the extent and issues of health care access and the health concern of Sri Lankan Tamil camp living refugees in Thiruvannamalai. For the study, one camp from Thiruvannamalai district was selected purposively. The selected camp is located in a rural area. Due to the restriction in entering the camp, the interview was conducted outside of the camps and respondents are selected through the convenience sampling method. Thirty camp inmates were interviewed with the help of a semi-structured interview schedule. The study revealed that the location of the camp is one of the major determinants of health care access. The people living in the camp of rural area can travel long hours to access health care. The government health care services to refugees are inadequate and improper. There is a delay in receiving the benefit of health care schemes and procedure of application is complicated. Besides, refugees are manual labours and they remain unemployed in half of every month. Therefore, the problem of affordability came into existence. An intervention on the part of the government is required to facilitate adequate health care services and health insurance should be extended to refugees.

Keywords: *Health care services, accessibility, the refugee crisis, health concern, camp life.*

Introduction

India has a long relationship with Sri Lanka as it is the neighbouring country located 20 miles away from the southern tip of India. During the 19th century, British East India Company hired Tamil labours from Tamil Nadu to work in the coffee and tea plantations in Sri Lanka. The labours bought from India are settled in the north-eastern parts of Sri Lanka. Sri Lankan population comprises of mostly Buddhist population. The Tamils from India are Hindus and are called later known as Sri Lankan Tamils. Seeds of the conflict were sown following independence from the United Kingdom in 1948, soon after which the new government of the Sinhalese-dominated United National Party disenfranchised Tamil plantation workers; the Sinhalese majority stoked more antagonism when it made Sinhala, rather than ethnic-neutral English, the national language in 1956, and promoted policies that further disenfranchised the Tamil minority (Berkley Center for Religion, Peace, and World Affairs, 2013). Tensions erupted in armed conflict in 1983, with the Black July riots that claimed the lives of thousands while the secular-nationalist LTTE launched attacks claiming both military and civilian lives. Lack of security in their home countries makes them seek asylum in another country. Lack of facilities in the countries of asylum leaves them frustrated with a low quality of life. To a refugee, the most important thing is to be alive, and so being alive takes precedence over their quality of life. Most of these refugees have fled over time leaving all that they had built in their lifetime and that of their ancestors.

Having left all their belongings back in their home country, refugees also leave behind their self-esteem, self-confidence, identity, dreams for the future, etc. When they reached the shores of India, many of them were not only without worldly belongings but also lacked the spirit. The difficulties they faced at the port of entry, being herded into camps, the suspicious on-lookers stripped what little self-respect remained in them. Most of the refugees in the camps do not live they just exist. Yet many have recuperated and have done wonders with whatever little that they have. The young refugees go to school and college; the older ones work and save for the day when they will be back in their country.

India is standing as a fast-growing country and one of the democratic countries in the world which does not have a refugee integration strategy. The needs of asylum seekers and refugees are subsumed under those of minority ethnic groups which are currently best addressed through the domestic laws in an ad hoc manner. So far in the case of Sri Lankan Tamil refugees, the common factors such as language, religion and ethnicity played a significant role in integration. Indian Tamils are most generous towards Sri Lankan Tamil Refugees and both state and central government have extended support to refugees during the ethnic conflict and since. On the arrival, all refugees are registered and accommodated in a transit camp. Later, shifted to various government-run camps and are provided with facilities of shelter, food, water supply, electricity, sanitation and health care. Also, monthly financial assistance, clothes, vessels, free education and various pensions and assistance are provided. These schemes have a significant impact on integrating refugees with the host society. It was in 1991 the former India Prime Minister Rajeev Gandhi assassinated by LTTE, a Tamil separatist organisation in Sri Lanka has created an atmosphere of dread and caused disintegration. Sri Lankan Tamils are arrested and imprisoned and local people keep a distance from refugees due to presence of militants among refugees. The assassination of former India president is the main reason that wipes out the sympathy and affinity. Since 1991 refugees are living with some degree of restrictions and are away from local settlements. Refugees are allowed to work, provided with free education, health care and all other benefits enjoyed the local community except citizenship.

The settlement in the camp has initially cured the wounds. But the camp life was like confinement and their socio-economic and living condition is dilapidated. Women deals with the problem of ill health, lack of privacy, sexual exploitation and mental stress. The atmosphere is not conducive to develop the socio-economic status. The assassination of Rajiv Gandhi by the LTTE and the fear of terrorism among refugees in India have resulted in the imposition of strict restriction especially in freedom of movement, education and other human rights. Later, the situation has been changed and the degree of restriction has slowly removed. The women are permitted to work and provide education, free of cost by the government. The access to job nearby camp is very difficult for women. The poor economic status has induced many women to seek employment away from the camp. The healthcare requirements of women are not met properly. Pregnant and aged women faced difficulty in accessing health care due to the remote location of the camp. On the course of time, the government has introduced numerous policies for the welfare of the refugees which facilitate the socio-economic development of refugee women. The schemes for education, marriage, healthcare, skill training and employment are very relevant in contributing the upliftment women refugees. Importantly, the implementation of SHGs in the camps has empowered sections of women by providing facilities for cottage industries, marketing business and agriculture activities. The refugees have marked progress in the socio-economic indicators along with integration in the host society which has accelerated the process of empowerment.

Methodology

The refugee camps in Tamil Nadu numbered 108 are scattered across the state. Since 1983, there is a sum of 3,04,269 refugees arrived in four phases. Now 63,351 refugees are living government camps and a 37,268 are non-camp refugees. The total number of families living in the camps is 19451. The non-camp refugees have the freedom to settle anywhere in Tamil Nadu and have the right to work away from their settlement but they need to register the local police station near to their place of living. The non-camp refugees cannot avail the benefit of government welfare schemes. The study only considered camp living refugees who are suffering from the problems of affordability and accessibility of basic healthcare due to the several factors which are treated as barriers.

Two camps are selected purposively for the study. Kasthambadi camp in Tiruvannamalai district was selected. Kasthambadi camp is located around 30 km away from Polur town. The location of this camp is extremely rural where most of the basic facilities are scarce. The camp inmates are engaged in agriculture works, painting, tailoring, concrete work and masonry, loading work and laying underground cable. Most of the camp inmates work as manual labours in various fields for the daily wage which is available only for a few days in a month.

The outsiders are not allowed to enter the camp. Therefore, the interview was done outside of the camps. A semi-structured schedule was used to interview the refugees when they going out of the camps. Those refugees sitting nearby tea shops and bus stops were met and a detailed interview was carried out. A sum of 20 refugees was interviewed from this camp. The respondents are selected based on the convenience of the researcher. The questions related to the availability, accessibility and affordability are asked to the respondents. Also, the basic socio-economic details are gathered. The qualitative research design was adopted for the study. The collected data was analysed with the help of SPSS and tabulated for camp wise comparison. The interview mainly focused on three main areas: accessibility, availability and affordability of healthcare facilities which are regarded as the main barriers of healthcare. In addition to field data, the study partly relays on reports of Commissioner of Rehabilitation and Welfare of Non-Resident Tamils, Government of Tamil Nadu.

Living Condition of Refugees

Life in the refugee camp is remarkably mistreated in nature and camps shift extraordinarily in size and personal satisfaction. Women in the camp endured a lot than male. There are no appropriate latrine facility in the camp. Indeed, even in a couple of toilets, water facilities are not given. Subsequently, people need to go open area or close-by forest to defecate. Due to the act of such non-existent practice in Sri Lankan culture, women endured a ton. Women go out to calm themselves; they confront prodding issues in a few zones (TN & PUCL, 2006) or individuals in adjacent crapping zone hit them with stones. Another issue that women face in the camp is deficiency of drinking water. In a few camps, open taps and well are developed by government and NGOs yet water comes just for a brief period. Women need to make a trip long distance to bring water.

There is no work allows in India, even though refugees who are conceded habitation licenses to find work in the casual area. Low wage, segregation in wage and misuse by the business is extremely basic among women labourers. For women who can find work in remote areas as household helps through an outside system of refugees, however, they are not ready to accept these open doors because of the confinements to their right side of development far from the camp. Sri Lankan Tamils have been conceded opportunity of development inside the camp territories, empowering work facilities for them as easygoing work. For a single-headed family, women have the monetary duty are subjected to wage work. The nonappearance of land, domesticated animals and properties, actuate them to subordinate altogether on nearby work advertise. The accessibility of business relies on the area of the camp. On the off chance that evacuees acquire work far from the camp and need to remain around there for several days, subsequently, they are in the danger of losing enlistment at the camp. Thus, the refugees are kept in the camps which augment the issue of economic backwardness.

Psychological stress because of the partition of family and the passing of relatives is basic among women in the camp. At least one individual has kicked the bucket is missing from one family. Now and again relatives are dispersed over various camps and their unification required significant investment. Inside the camp, life is truly hopeless since the death of Rajiv Gandhi, the previous executive of India by an associated part with the LTTE. The strict rules of authorities have increased mental and compassionate issues. Food shortage and malnutrition issues are normal in prior days and nourishment grains gave to them are of low quality. Besides, they don't approach an agreeable place to rest or great sustenance. Separation and maltreatment by authorities and nearby individuals are common in their day by day life (Drishti, 2015). In like manner, stringent confinement, exploitation and racial segregation by specialists are high in camps. They are under twenty-four hours reconnaissance of the security officers and opportunity of exit was limited between 6.00 A.M to 6.00 P.M inconsistently. The government has been sans giving restorative treatment from government healing centres and PHCs. Health workers and medicinal officers regularly visit the camps and give fundamental treatment. In any case, the infections, for example, tuberculosis, typhoid and looseness of the bowels are predominant. Access to medicinal offices are another issue, in light of numerous camps are situated far from urban regions where restorative offices are accessible. Countless particularly women displaced people have experiencing issues identified with psychological wellness.

Barriers in Health Care: Accessibility, Availability and Affordability

Availability and accessibility of services depend upon the nature of area or location. In urban areas, basic services are available very easily and which are abundant in nature. For example, the number of hospitals, educational institutions and transportation facilities is higher urban areas. Therefore, the question of availability and accessibility is ruled out. As far as the rural area is concerned, the basic services are very poor and scarce. The development of the service sector is very low in rural areas but agriculture is the dominant sector.

The accessibility and availability of healthcare services for refugees are provided by government and NGOs. The government has been providing free health services in government hospitals for refugees. Poor sanitation, the lake of water and free space, limited access to healthcare facilities are the persistent problems in the refugee camps of Tamil Nadu (Bai, 2005). The initial period of the influx of refugees to Tamil Nadu, the government has provided health services to refugees within the camp and appointed healthcare professionals who have visited the camp and monitor the health status of refugees. It is reported by the Refugees Council, London, (1999) that there was a higher prevalence of diseases such as tuberculosis, typhoid, and diarrhoea in several camps. Moreover, a large number of refugees are suffering from problems related to mental health. Unfortunately, most of the camps are located in remote areas; therefore it is very difficult to find healthcare services away from the camp (The Refugee Council, London, 1999). The accessibility, availability and affordability have varied by location of the camp.

The respondents from Kasthambadi camp in Thiruvannamalai district argued that they have higher access to private healthcare facilities than public healthcare. The government hospital in this area lacks healthcare infrastructures such as labs, staff and beds. Therefore, refugees are either preferring Government Medical College in Chennai, Vellore and Tiruvallur districts. It is observed that many camp refugees had undergone surgeries in this medical college free of cost and the government has provided Rs. 15000 for those who are subjected to surgery.

Rural refugees are facing severe problems in accessing basic healthcare services. In rural, the main occupation is agriculture (UNHCR, 2018) and their ability to seek high-cost medical treatment away from the place is comparatively low due to poor financial stability. Low accessibility, availability and affordability of healthcare services are the main problems in rural areas. It is found that rural refugees either to move urban areas or prefer local clinic, PHCs and Government hospitals for treatment. For major surgeries, they should go to hospitals in urban areas. The respondents mentioned that the rural location of the camp has hampered the socio-economic development. In the Kasthambadi Camp (rural camp), a private clinic is located five kilometer away from the camp and a government hospital is around 10 kilometer away. These services are inadequate to meet the needs of deliveries and heavy injuries. In these cases, they preferred government hospitals in Tiruvannalai, vellur and Chennai districts. It is noted the poor economic background has induced them to choose government hospitals, their healthcare is free including surgeries. It is pinpoint that the government has appointed healthcare staff to provide health treatment to ill persons in the camp who are working in the PHCs. If any health issues reported in the camp, the health worker will visit and provide medical attention. Also, some NGOs are providing healthcare services. It is, therefore, summarised that rural refugees have limited access to healthcare facilities and the availability of healthcare is very low. The economic backwardness causes the problem of affordability. The complete healthcare of rural refugees is remained unachieved due to the improper setting of the healthcare system. Therefore, an initiative from the part of the government is required to facilitate healthcare to refugees in rural areas.

A refugee aged 60, stated that "*I am suffering from old age problems and some injuries from civil in Sri Lanka still affecting my health. The absence of proper healthcare facilities nearer has induced me to travel long or remain ill without any treatment.*" Practical hindrances obstruct access to health-care services for refugees like deficient information and mindfulness about the availability of services, lacking money related means, confined access to transport, socially cold-hearted care, and insufficient arrangement of helpers. Besides, poor access to health-care services associates with segregation and constrained social rights in this manner strengthening avoidance as the main driver of sick wellbeing among refugees in the rural area.

Conclusion

Several barriers retard the refugees to access health care in the host. The location of the camp is very significant in this regard. The remote location of the camp causes the problem of accessibility of better healthcare to the refugees. The poor earnings of the refugees are not enough to meet the expenditure of advance health care and other related expenses. Private medical services are many costs for refugees. The provision of free health care under the public sector is inadequate in the region. Therefore, the refugees have to travel a long distance to access public healthcare services. The camp restriction is not a barrier in accessing healthcare services. The healthcare barriers to the refugees are mainly associated with the nature of the area of their settlement.

The Indian government has implemented specific schemes for refugees to ensure their well-being. In addition to what has already been underlined, the Indian government has several times implemented schemes for such refugees. For instance, in 2012, the Tamil Nadu Chief Minister Jayalalitha ordered extension of the government's comprehensive health insurance scheme to Sri Lankan Tamil refugees; a scheme initially targeting poor people in the state was extended to them. Through the years Tamil Nadu has decided to contribute actively to the welfare of Sri Lankan Tamil refugees within the state by giving them certain access to benefits established for Indian nationals as well as contributing to their well-being. The health of the refugees is always a concern of the government. But the barriers exist in rural camps in a large extent due to the geographical isolation of the camp location from the mainstream population. The government should extend the healthcare services to rural areas with advance facilities to solve the problems associated with accessibility, availability and affordability.

References

- Ahmad Zarin (2001) Ethnic conflict and refugee: A case study of Sri Lankan. Ph. D., thesis submitted to the Jawaharlal Nehru University. http://shodhganga.inflibnet.ac.in/handle/10603/108796. Date accessed: 20/10/2016
- Asha Hans (1993) Sri Lankan Tamil refugees in India, *refuge*, 13 (3) 30-33
- Bastiampillai Bertram (1994) Sri Lankan Tamil Refugees in Tamil Nadu: Trouble to the Host. Paper presented at the international seminar on refugees and internal security in South Asia. http://repository.forcedmigration.org/pdf/?pid=fmo:1246. Date accessed: 25/10/2016.

- Bhalla Nita, (2014) Five years after the war, Sri Lanka refugees reluctant to leave India-survey. http://news.trust.org//item/20141029085451-ru1cx/. Date accessed: 25/10/2016.
- Chaterjee Patralekha, (2003) Tales from Tamil refugee camps. http://www.redcross.int/EN/mag/magazine1997_3/20-21.html. Date accessed: 28/11/2016.
- Daniel Pepper, (2006) Tamils fleeing war in Sri Lanka find refuge in India's southeast/About 16,000 people have entered the camps since January. November 20, 2006. http://www.sfgate.com/news/article/Tamils-fleeing-war-in-Sri-Lanka-find-refuge-in-2545953.php. Date accessed: 19/11/2016

  Date accessed: 04/08/2016
- Drishti, (2015) Conflict, Refugee Situation and Human Rights: A Case Study of Tamil Refugees in the Sri Lankan Conflict, http://www.lawctopus.com/academike/conflict-refugee-situation-and-human-rights-a-case-study-of-tamil-refugees-in-the-sri-lankan-conflict. Date Accessed: 04/10/2016
- http://shodhganga.inflibnet.ac.in/handle/10603/108796. Date accessed: 25/10/2016
- Janardhanan Arun, (2015) Explained: The Sri Lankan Refugee Question. http://indianexpress.com/article/india/india-others/explained-the-sri-lankan-refugee-question/. /. Date accessed: 22/10/2016.
- Jayapalan Athithan, (2012) Refugees Status and citizenship, Sri Lankan Refugees in India. Refugee Watch, 117-120. http://www.mcrg.ac.in/rw%20files/RW39_40/9.pdf.
- Kalnad Nayan, Niranjan Bose and Hari Menon (2017) India's great healthcare challenge, also an opportunity. http://www.hindustantimes.com/india-news/india-s-great-healthcare-challenge-and-opportunity/story-eB691Pj889x57TYo8MobaM.html. Date accessed: 10/08/2017.
- Kathirgamathamby, Y., (2015) Voluntary Repatriation as a Durable Solution to Sri Lankan Refugees in India: A Critical Analysis with Legal Perspective, Proceedings of 8th International Research Conference, KDU, Published November 2015.
- Mathew, (2016) A flight by Sri Lankan Tamil refugees demanding freedom and opportunities in India. The News Minute. August 1, 2016. http://www.thenewsminute.com/article/fight-sri-lankan-tamil-refugees-demanding-freedom-and-opportunities-india-47466. Date accessed: 10/05/2016
- Miriam George (2013) Sri Lankan Tamil refugee experience: A qualitative analysis, *International Journal of Culture and Mental Health*, 6(3), 170-182.
- Natarajan Swaminathan (2007) War-weary Tamils face India hardship. BBC News. 4 June 2007. http://news.bbc.co.uk/2/hi/south_asia/6708947.stm. Date accessed: 20/11/2016

- Parivelan, K. M., (2015) Exploring Durable Solution for Sri Lankan Refugees in India. Regional Cooperation Newsletter-South Asia. October 2014 – April 2015, 2-10.
- PUCL Bulletin (2006) Conditions in Sri Lankan Tamil refugee camps. TN & Pondicherry PUCL report, 18 June 2006. http://www.pucl.org/Topics/International/2006/refugees-srilanka-report.html. Date Accessed: 31/05/2017.
- Raizada Himanshi (2013) Sri Lankan Refugees in India: The Problem and the Uncertainty. *International Journal of Peace and Development.* 1(1), 01-29
- Refugees International, (2004) forgotten people: Upcountry Tamils from Sri Lanka living in refugee camps in India. 15 Sep 2004. http://reliefweb.int/report/sri-lanka/forgotten-people-upcountry-tamils-sri-lanka-living-refugee-camps-india. Date accessed: 20/11/2016
- Roberts, J. Marc (2011) Pharmaceutical Reform: A Guide to Improving Performance and Equity. p.220. https://books.google.com/books?id=mT7ImUC6A7kC&pg= PA220&lpg= PA220&dq. Date accessed: 19/08/2017.
- Sakthivel, G., (2016) the socio-economic conditions of Sri Lankan Tamil refugees in Tamil Nadu. 2(6), pp. 1-5.
- Sengupta Arpita, (2014) Sri Lankan Tamil Refugees in India: will they be granted citizenship? *Refugee Watch Online.* http://refugeewatchonline.blogspot.in.
- Sri Lanka Guardian, (2008) Home is a refugee camp in Tamil Nadu. http://www.srilankaguardian.org/2008/07/home-is-refugee-camp-in-tamil-nadu.html. Date Accessed: 05/09/2016.
- Sudha Ramalingam, (2000) A report on Conditions in Refugee Camp in Vellore, Tamil Nadu. People's Union of Civil Liberties Tamil Nadu & Pondicherry, 23 August 2000. http://tamilnation.co/refugees/00vellore.htm. Date accessed: 15/11/2016
- Suryanarayan, R (2003) Humanitarian concerns and security needs: Sri Lankan refugees in Tamil Nadu (edi.), Chari P.R, Joseph Mallika and Chandra Suba (2003) Missing Boundaries, 39-59, Manohar Publisher, New Delhi.
- Suryanarayan, V., (2015) Focus on the Sri Lankan Tamil refugees. http://www.srilankaguardian.org/2009/11/fo cus-on-Sri-Lankan-Tamil-refugees.html. Date Accessed: 27/11/2016.
- The Refugee Council, London (1999) The Sri Lanka Project. Sri Lankan refugees in the Indian state of Tamil Nadu. August 1999
- Thuppahi's Blog, (2012) Lankan Tamil refugees in India and their repatriation. IRIN News item, 30 August 2012. https://thuppahi.wordpress.com/2012/08/30/lankan-tamil-refugees-in-india-and-their-repatriation/. Date accessed: 19/11/2016
- Valatheeswaran, C., (2014) Living condition of Sri Lankan Tamil refugees in India. Irudaya Rajan. S (edit) India Migration Report

2014- Diaspora and Development. Pp. 287-299. Routledge Publishers, New Delhi.

- Valatheeswaran, C., and Irudaya Rajan, S., (2011) Sri Lankan Tamil Refugees in India: Rehabilitation Mechanisms, Livelihood Strategies, and Lasting Solutions. *Refugee Survey Quarterly*. 30(2), 24-44.
- Virmani, Shipra (2014) Population - as an asset or liability. International Journal of Computing and Corporate Research, 4(6), 1-7. https://www.ijccr.com/November2014/9.pdf. Date accessed: 10/08/2017.
- Xavier Gladston, and Florin Benoit, (2011) security among the refugees and quality of life-case of the Sri Lankan Tamil refugees living in camps in Tamil Nadu. *Refugee Watch*, 37, 1-15.

13

Health Issues & Problems of Working Women

— Dr. Ch. Radhika,
Dr. N. Sai Babu

God has gifted women with compassion, tender-heartedness, caring nature, concern for others. These are very positive signs which imply that women can be leaders. In order to help women to be in limelight, they need to be empowered. If we take a look at the history, we come to know there is a mountain of efforts behind the success of woman. Still, she has to go a long way. It has provided on kind of support to women empowerment not only in India, but also in the world around. It was a very long way to go for a women. She has struggled a lot to acquire the present position. Women bear almost all responsibilities for meeting basic needs of the family, yet are systematically denied the resources, information and freedom of action they need to fulfill this responsibility. In India position of woman differs. She has to fight against many forces, such as gender discrimination, racial discrimination, caste, colour and the orthodox social norms. It is an open truth that working women have to face problems just by virtue of their being women.

To acquire women empowerment, women have undergone unbelievable sufferings, lots of obstacles, struggle, resistance and changes. Literally she has walked on fire and took many challenges. Still she is fighting with the social evils. Although she has overcome numerous difficulties, she can never be used as commodity by male-chauvinism and other repressive forces, which were responsible for her marginalization. Regarding Indian women, A.R. Desai observes:

> The subjugation of Indian women in the Pre-British period was rooted in the social and economic structure of society of the period. (1989: 247)

Technological advancement results in retrenchment of women employees. No one thinks of upgrading their skills. Women going to work are often subject to sexual harassment. The psychological pressure of all this can easily lead to a woman quitting her job. Most of the problems that beset working women are in reality rooted in the social perspective of the position of women. Traditionally men are seen as the bread winner and women as the house-keepers and child bearers. This typecast role model continues to put obstacles before the working women. A fundamental change is required in the attitudes of the employers, policy makers, family members and other relatives and the public at large. In ancient times things were not favorable to women to cross the door steps and to find her place in the main stream. They were oppressed, subjugated and marginalized for centuries as they happen to live in a male dominant society and were denied chance to express themselves. They have undergone so many orders in their life. In spite of which they have failed to attain freedom, liberty and equality on par with men. Woman as a creatrix with immense possibilities. A bird cannot fly on one wing. So our society needs to develop womanhood to its fullest extent. Otherwise society ruins itself. As wife and mother in the home, she is seldom given due recognition and her worth and services are taken for granted.

For centuries together she was projected in such a way that she was physically, mentally and intellectually weak. In this context we have to redefine, re-read and rewrite the popular saying of Shakespeare "Women thy name is frailty". This saying doesn't suit to the modern times as the women are excelling in all walks of life that is stating from the lowest status of a sarpanch to that of securing a berth in space. Such is the power and glory of Indian women in recent times.

This paper mainly focuses on health issues and problems of the working women. Women not only have to keep proving their worth at work constantly but also juggle around their personal and social lives so as to not let them affect their professional life. Working conditions and environment can have a huge impact on mental health and, equally, someone's mental health can have a significant impact on their ability to perform well in their job.

A woman is entitled to live in dignity and in freedom from want and from fear. Empowering women is also an indispensable tool for advancing development and reducing poverty. Empowered women contribute to the health and productivity of whole families and communities and to improve prospects for the next generation. When a woman can plan her family, she can plan the rest of her life. When she is healthy, she can be more productive. And when her reproductive rights — including the right to decide the number, timing and spacing of her children, and to make decisions regarding reproduction free of discrimination, coercion and violence are promoted and protected, she has freedom to participate more fully and equally in society.

We've come a long way since 1995 and it is time to exult women and their feat. But it is also time to take stock of how women's rights are fulfilled in the world — especially the right to health. Twenty years after countries signed pledges in the 1995 Beijing Declaration and Platform of Action, women still face many health problems and we must re-commit to addressing them. According to a press release, the study found that 78 per cent of the sample size suffered from lifestyle, chronic and acute ailments. These included obesity, depression, chronic backache, diabetes, hypertension, high cholesterol, heart and kidney diseases.

Striking the accurate symmetry between work and home has always been a challenge for working women. This survey uncover that daily "multi-tasking" is taking a levy on their health. The worst part is most of the pretentious women are in between 32 to 58 age group.

Economic independence is a windfall for females. Working women can take their own decisions, live life as per their expectations and enjoy freedom of spending. However, you fail to notice the struggle or adverse effect on health. Due to the hectic lifestyle, work load, added responsibilities, menopause or hormonal changes, working women suffer more than working men. For working women it is complicated to sustain personal and professional life which results into various health problems. Here I would like to discuss ten of the main issues regarding women's health.

1. **Cancer:** Two of the most common cancers that affect women are breast and cervical cancers. Identifying both these cancers early is solution to keep women alive and healthy. Especially working women will get cervical cancer because of the unhygienic conditions of the bathrooms at work places. The latest global figures show that around half a million women die from cervical cancer and half a million from breast cancer each year.
2. **Maternal health:** Due to the work pressure at office, many of the working women will not get the sufficient time to take the proper care during pregnancy and childbirth. It may leads to Asthma, diabetes and depression. It can harm the mother and child during pregnancy if not managed

properly. Due to this almost 30000 women died from complication in pregnancy and childbirth in 2013.

3. **Violence against women:** Women can be subjected to a range of different forms of violence, but physical and sexual violence – either by a partner or someone else – is particularly unpleasant. In some cases working women face this problem from her husband every month after she got her salary. Men vigorously seize the salary from his wife and not even bother about her personal needs. If she discards to give the salary, husband will threaten or beat her literally. This kind of violence affects their physical and mental health in the short and long-term. Many women suffer psychological abuse (such as humiliation and verbal degradation) from the partners,
4. **Mental health:** Work pressures both at home and office makes her restless and it leads to her depression. Due to late night work and changing shifts along with stressful schedules, she even can't get the proper sleep at night. Sleep deprivation causes other health problems. Evidence suggests that women are more prone than men to experience anxiety, depression and somatic complaints – physical symptoms that cannot be explained medically. Depression is the most common mental health problem for women and sometimes it leads to suicide.
5. **Obesity:** Sedentary lifestyle, lack of exercise and poor eating habits are main reasons for increasing obesity, it leads to PCOD, diabetes and related problems.
6. **Hypertension:** Stressful working conditions, less time to relax and certain medical factors increase the risk of hypertension. Hypertension along with diabetes can cause further health issues.

7. **Stroke:** Lifestyle negligence is mainly responsible for health problems. Now-a-days heart problems starts from age of 35 years.
8. **Musculoskeletal Issues:** Chronic back pain or neck pain is one of the common problems amongst working women.
9. **Female Sexual Arousal Disorder (FSAD):** Many working women complain of losing interest in sex. Though they may want to enjoy sex, they suffer from FSAD, due to fatigue, lack of sleep and stress. This can adversely affect their relation with their partners also.
10. **Work – life balance**: Working women tend to be like a pendulum clock oscillating between work demands and home household tasks. Between these oscillations, there are social expectations to match up to and the constant anxiety of keeping up with demands of both the worlds. Most women find themselves juggling errands at home and outside, adding to the workload and emotional burden. At the same time, at home, a woman is expected to continue fulfilling her 'natural' duties as a mother and wife, and is put under extra scrutiny when she chooses to work outside the house. The combination of juggling caring commitments for children and family as well as doing paid work and facing physical health problems could increase the risk of experiencing mental distress.
11. **Gender bias:** Gender bias creates an obstacle at the recruitment stage itself. When it comes to remuneration the law proclaims equality but it is seldom put into practice. The inbuilt conviction is that women are capable of less work than men or less efficient. Gender based constrictions are factor that inhibit men's or women's access to resources, rights, behavior, participation and exercise of power

based on their gender identity. These constraints result in exploitation, violence, denial, isolation, melancholy and complete attrition of self worth. Even though, women is capable enough the management at the workplace denies the women to held higher positions. Unequal treatment of women and men also creates distress in working women.

12. **Malnourishment:** Undernourishment among women in India is high. In the Global Hunger index calculated by IFPRI (2008), India ranks 66th among 88 ranks. India also scores 23.7 with an 'alarming' hunger incidence. (Gandhi: 2009) Women's nutritional levels are lower than men since women face discrimination right from the time of breastfeeding to their adulthood. (Pandey : 2009) Thus, nutritional and psychological problems also have a profound effect upon their health status.
13. **Maternity Leave:** It is seldom given. It is much easier to terminate the woman's employment and hire someone else. This will directly effect on her mind and creates a kind of depression.

Women going to work are often subjected to sexual harassment. Public transport system is overcrowded and men take advantage of the circumstances to physically harass women. Colleagues offer unwanted attention which can still be shaken off but a woman is placed in a difficult situation if the higher officer demands sexual favours. The psychological pressure of all this can easily lead to a woman quitting her job. Most of the problems that beset working women are in reality rooted with social perspective of the position of women. Traditionally men are seen as the bread winner and women as the house-keepers, child bearers and rearers. This typecast role model continues to put obstacles before the working women. A fundamental change is required in the attitudes of the employers, policy makers, family members and other relatives and the public at large. It is an undeniable fact that in this 20th century the status of women has definitely risen up compared to that of the past. But it is also a reality that even now a woman has not become independent. She faces a lot of problems especially the working women. According to Mira

> The conditions of married working women is still worse since she has to play a dual role; that of a house wife and of employed women. (1998)

There are contradictory role expectations from working women while she is at work and at home.

> On professional front she is expected to be dedicated, vibrant, competitive, straight forward, non-sentimental and act in a "business like" manner and at home, she is expected to be sweet, soft, sensitive, adaptable, gentle, unassertive and domesticated. (Misra 1998: 15).

These paradoxical expectations cause the most bewilderment, anxiety and generate many other problems for her. A woman employee locates it complicated to do fairness to the two roles at the same time. Maintenance of satisfactory family relationship: There is another problematic area for working woman. As Goode points out,

> The modern industrial world is the first cultural system to permit woman to occupy independent jobs. Thus woman may have a "better bargaining position within the family system and increase their say in decision making. This brings about changes in the traditional family role relationships. (1968: 72)

Care giving and family responsibilities, economic insecurity and experiences of violence and abuse are common for working women. All these factors exert a negative impact on the health status of Indian women. According to Parikh

> For women, the 'spillover' of family related stress on work related stress is higher than it is in the case of men. (2004: 125)

The work place can also be a site where women are subjected to sexual violence and gender discrimination. As Kaila writes,

> Research evidence indicates that women face certain work related health problems such as psychosomatic symptoms, general health and women specific health problems, including menstrual disorder, anxiety, backache, anemia, depression, abortion, miscarriage and other gynecological problems. (2004: 4)

The Vedas said **"Matru Devo Bhava"**-revere our mother as God. We must revere our mother who has brought us up with love, care and sacrifice. The healthy and wealthy nation can be build up only through healthy children who are born from the womb of healthy mammals. Hence it is the responsibility of every one to provide sufficient and essential nutritious food to mammal, children and women to see a cheerful and glorious world.

It needs to attain support from various other dimensions like policies of the state and central government, Nutrition and health, Leadership and employment opportunities. Even though women are working and independent most women do not have autonomy in decision making in their personal lives. Workplaces are often unwilling or unable to provide the flexibility women need, which also plays a role in affecting their mental health. Women should have their own social circle. They should care for themselves. They should believe that the world is at their feet and sky is the limit for their progress and development.

In the coming years we can expect a swifter change in the roles women play in all spheres and this will surely transform the face of the world. Let us expect a world where women are not treated as puppets but as human beings, a world where women are not treated weaker class but as counter parts, a world where woman are not denied freedom but have equal rights, a just world – a living world.

Women are sure to leap across the gender divide and take charge to empower themselves on a mega-scale.

All over the world women continue to concentrate in less skilled, lower paid jobs and are still a minority in most of the managerial positions. In every part of the world, women have always worked since the beginning of human life on the earth. But in a male-dominant society like India, they are always being questioned about their intelligence, skill, capability, ambitions and performance as mangers. The very next task and challenge will be to develop their capacity so that they can perform their role properly and can make a difference.

Works Cited

- Gandhi, C. 2009. *Alarming poverty in India: Global Hunger Index.*
- Goode, WJ. 1968. *World Revolution and Family Patterns.* New York: The Free Press.
- Kaila, H.L. 2004. Editorial. *Journal of Health Management* Special Issue on *Occupational health of women,* Vol. 6. No. 2. pp. 3-5.
- Messias, DKH, et al. 1997. "Defining and redefining work: Implications for women's health." *Gender and Society.* Vol. 11. No. 3. p. 296-323.
- Misra, Pushpa (1998). Predictors of Work-Family Conflict among Indian Women. Indian Journal of Psychology. Vol. 25. No. 1. p. 13-19.
- Pandey, A. 2009. *Gender Differences in Early Childhood Feeding Practices: Rural West Bengal. Gender and Discrimination: Health, Nutritional Status and Women in India.* Edited by M. Pal, et al. New Delhi: Oxford University Press, p. 186-206.
- Parikh, J. 2004. "Occupational Stress and Coping among Nurses." *Journal of Health Management* (Special Issue on Occupational Health of Women), Vol. 6. No. 2. p. 115-127.

14

New Reproductive Technology: Towards a Feminists Perspective

— ***Papari Kalita***

Abstract

By examining women's health through feminists lens one can understand the gender relations in the society. The expansion of medical profession and medical technologies have introduced a wide range of medical intervention into new areas of women's health and New Reproductive Technology is such an expansion of medical technology which have been the subject of heated debate among feminists, academics, medical ethicists and policy makers. A feminist oriented assessment of this reproductive technology is much needed as the matter is not fertility here, the actual matter is the exploitation of women. The development, consolidation and amplification of Assisted Reproductive Technology (ART) as a different group of procedure designed to assist conception by correcting or bypassing infertility is comparatively recent. The largely privatized infertility care clinic treated childlessness as 'abnormal', stigmatizes infertility and is based on the understanding that a woman can only become 'complete' by becoming mother and thus strengthens the patriarchal norms of motherhood. The socio-cultural and patriarchal values are used by the medical market to promote ARTs. The non-biological contexts of infertility are given minimal importance by the medical professionals, their response to infertility has become increasingly technological and emphasized on surgical intervention. This paper attempts to view ART from feminist point of view, consider the social, economical and ethical issues involved with it and to determine whether the choices of women to undergo ART treatment lead to their emancipation or it further impair their situation.

Keywords: *Infertility, Gender, Reproductive Technology, Motherhood, Emancipation*

In simple term, Assisted Reproductive Technologies (ARTs) refer to those development of technologies which assist reproduction but in reality, it has a far more greater connotations than simply assist reproduction and those connotations are bring into light by the feminists who viewed these development with suspicion and because of whom the issue become heated debate among many. Feminism has historically provided the major challenge to normative conceptions about health and body, reciprocally the issue of health has been a crucial vehicle for the development of feminist theory dating back to at least the eighteenth century (Annandale, 2009). Ellen Lewin and Virginia Olesen had made a statement that an examination of health is revealing of such elements of culture and society which has a direct bearing on the construction of gender and its consequences for women, men and the larger social order (Lewin, 1985). Therefore an examination of women's health from a feminist perspective is crucial in the understanding of gender relations in a society (Sahin, 2016).

Women's health is an issue which receives less concern from feminist and also in general, even the first wave feminist didn't want to focus on women's health as they believed that focusing on health or body will differentiate women from men. In India, women's health was focused upon after the International community recognized it as an area of major concern for development. The program of Action adopted by 176 countries in the UN Cairo Conference in 1994 saw for the first time, the reproductive and sexual health and the rights of women become a central element in an international agreement on population and development (Mathur, 2008). Although women's health became an area of concern, yet as a site of inquiry, reproduction is a late entrant in the social sciences (Marwah & Sarojini N, 2011). The issue of reproduction is considered as purely private and therefore no one tried to question it. Much of the credit for destabilising this notion, in addition to dismantling similar "sealed-off" ways to looking at the body, goes to feminist thought (Rapp, 2001).

'Technologically assisted reproduction' is not a new phenomenon, yet the development and consolidation of ARTs as a distinct group of procedures designed to assist conception by correcting or circumventing infertility is relatively recent (Marwah & Sarojini N, 2011). ARTs include procedures such as, intra-uterine or artificial insemination (IUI), in-vitro fertilization (IVF), intracytoplasmic sperm injection (ICSI), embryo freezing etc. Surrogacy, which uses ARTs, although in itself it is an arrangement and not a technology, also falls within the ambit of ARTs (Marwah & Sarojini N, 2011). Those who rejects technology on the ground of being inherently patriarchal is of the view that reproduction is a 'natural' process over which men (seek to) exert control through technological intervention (Corea, 1985; Marwah & Sarojini N, 2011), others who are in favor of technology see reproductive technology as bearing the potential to liberate women by conquering reproductive biology, which has been the fundamental source of women's relegation to the private, domestic sphere of family (Firestone, 1971; Marwah & Sarojini N, 2011). Feminists International Network of Resistance to Reproductive and Genetic Engineering (FINRRAGE) stated that "these technologies then, at their core, are not only sexist, but racist, classist and deeply eugenic and serve as old and new instruments of population control" (Klein, 2008: 158).

Medical science and Promotion of ART

ARTs have been critically appraised for the patriarchal and capitalist agenda that lies at the heart of it, for promoting instead of questioning the power relations that equate motherhood with womanhood. Infertility affects more than 15% of all reproductive-aged couples worldwide at some point in their lives (Vayena et al. 2002). The scope and gravity of the infertility problem is much more severe in the non Western world, owing largely to the problem of untreated reproductive tract infections (Bentley & Mascie-Taylor, 2000; Brady 2003; Inhorn 2003a,b; Nachtigall 2006; Van Balen & Inhorn 2002), pelvic scarring, endometriosis, unsafe abortions and poor maternal healthcare, malnutrition, anaemia, low sperm count and the like. Through the use of effective infertility treatments these causes can be treated but medical professionals deal with these causes by simply circumventing it rather than curing it. From a historical perspective it is interesting that until the 1970s, infertility was most often seen as a psychosomatic problem, not amenable to medical intervention (Sandelowski, 1990; Strickler, 1992). The change in approach could be attributed to technological advances which have made medical treatment possible, or to demographic pressures which have forced obstetricians to seek out new markets for their service (Scritchfield, 1989; Strickler, 1992).

The focus of infertility specialists in response to infertility is to deliver a child to the infertile couple through medical interventions. With the exception of references to psychological disturbance and stress (Keye, 1984), medical literature rarely discusses the non biological context of infertility: the impact on a marriage, family relationships, career, or other aspect of everyday life (Strickler, 1992). The Indian Council for Medical Research (ICMR), in collaboration with World Health Organization (WHO), defines infertility as "the failure to conceive after at least one year of unprotected coitus". Till 1975, infertility holds the idea of unable to conceive up to five years of unprotected sex. In 1975, WHO minimizes the period to two years and in 2005, it was set to one year (Sama 2006:10). By defining infertility in terms of time and brought down the time to one year more and more people will fall under the definition and it helps the infertility specialist to declare a couple as 'infertile' , and they started medicalising their situation though there is a possibility to correct their infertility without any medical intervention.

New Reproductive Technologies: Boon or Curse

Gena Corea, member of the Feminist International Network Resisting Reproductive and Genetic Engineering (FINNRAGE) , with respect to ART explained that the issue is not fertility, the issue is the exploitation of women (Corea, 1985). The impact of ART on women's lives, the social construction of infertility and the objectification and personification of human through the purchase and sale reproductive material and organs have became the focus area of most feminist groups. The techniques of coercion inherent within the patriarchal system which play on women's lives when it comes to desiring children is also an underlying current in feminists discussion on the ART (Rowland, 1992; Corea, 1985; Sahin, 2016). ARTs have created a 'fertility market' where human reproductive parts like eggs, sperms, uteri and embryos can be 'bought', 'sold', or 'hired' (Marwah & Sarojini N, 2011). In most countries sale of organ is illegal but semen, ova, blood and other body fluids and tissues fall outside the purview of existing legislations because of their regenerative nature (Gupta & Richters, 2008; Marwah & Sarojini N, 2011). Thus, reproductive materials and organs become the income generating source for all those who are selling them. ART has transformed reproductive materials and organs into commodities which can be bought or sold in exchange of money, since the person who is selling them they have a right over these as it belongs to them Nobody questioned about the development of this business. There is a need to change in the terminology from "donor" to "seller".

Pregnancy is a natural process and women have certain natural rights in this process but all their rights have been taken away by the physician (infertility specialists) and they started to control the body and lives of the women. Women allow to occur all these without any interference only to get a biological child and to get the tagline "mother" on which society places a high premium. She is ostracized and stigmatized socially if she could not fulfill the demand of the society. Infertile couple could also adopt a child as a solution to their childlessness instead of undergoing surgical treatment but the idea of having a biological child who will carry their own genes is so much deeply attached in their thinking that they regarded adoption as a last option rather than considering it as an alternative. ART industry is growing based on this premise, the people who contributes in the development of ART they also form a part of the existing patriarchal social structure and therefore patriarchal values affect their construction of 'who is a woman'. 'Research findings have highlighted the fact that ARTs were promoting the idea that motherhood is woman's destiny, and capitalizing on the stigma and trauma of childlessness within marriage' (Marwah & Sarojini N, 2011).

Abdallah S. Daar, and Zara Merali made a statement, "Infertility in developing countries extends beyond the loss of human potential and *unrealized self*. The experience of infertility causes harsh, poignant, and unique difficulties: economic hardship, social stigma and blame, social isolation and alienation, guilt, fear, loss of social status, helplessness and, in some cases violence" (Daar & Merali, 2001). 'Infertility often produces a sense of isolation, resentment and anger which can lead to a vicious circle of cutting oneself off from social support networks' (Strickler, 1992).

Feminist Responses Towards ARTs

There has been feminist engagement with the issues of ARTs, they have criticized the increasing medicalisation of reproduction. Feminists have argued that these procreative technologies threaten women's role in procreation (Corea, 1985; Rothman, 1989). 'The investment in and emphasis on new technologies which facilitate biological parenthood reinforce the idea that women need to be mothers in order to feel fulfilled' (Strickler, 1992). 'Technological conception transfers reproductive control from women to physicians', women lose their control over conception as well as gestation (Strickler, 1992). 'To feminists, the problem is not a woman's inability to bear children (which is seen as an individual, not social, problem) but the structure and institutions of society which reinforce the necessity of child bearing for women's fulfillment on one hand, and physicians' increasing power in managing procreation on the other' (Strickler, 1992). Jennifer Strickler explained about four grounds on which the new procreative technology is attacked by feminists- 1) it takes reproductive control away from women and gives it to (mostly male) physicians, 2) it is physically and emotionally harmful to women, 3) it reinforces the importance of motherhood in women's lives, 4) it carries with it the potential for eugenic uses (Strickler, 1992).

There are feminists, who are in support of reproductive technology on the ground that it has 'extended reproductive rights to those who might remain otherwise childless. For example, they see them as a "solution" to *infertility* and thus beneficial to infertile couples; but they also see them as beneficial to those who are not involved in traditional heterosexual family situations or marriages. The arguments developed in favor of procreative rights support the rights of couples to reproduce in many different ways: coitally, noncoitally (AI, IVF), and noncoitally through the intermediacy of donors or surrogates' (Chokr, 1992).

Others have also argued that, 'ART has today created three possible mothers to a child. There is for one a 'genetic' mother- the woman responsible for providing the egg that is ultimately fertilized; the 'carrying' or gestational mother- the woman whose womb is used to carry the fetus until it develops to term; and finally the 'nurturing' or 'social' mother- the woman who perhaps commissioned the entire procreation contract and raises the child after it is born'

(Koyonda, 2001). Similarly, a sperm donor whose sperm is used to fertilize the egg of the wife of another man may rightfully claim to be the genetic father, but his role as legal and nurturing or social father after delivery is not exactly clear, this has leaves undefined the 'parents', and also leaves unsettled questions of parental rights and obligations of both parents and even the child (Koyonda, 2001).

Regulation of ART

To regulate the increased technological intervention in the area of reproduction which contributes in the development of a huge fertility market and to protect the rights and interest of the users of ART, the central government and the Indian Council of Medical Research (ICMR) have drafted the Assisted Reproductive Technologies (Regulation) Bill and Rules 2008. However, it is questionable whether the bill actually regulate the unregulated growth of these industries or it further promoting and protecting the interest of the private sector providers of these technologies. With regard to the risks associated with ART the bill states that "ART carry small risks both to the mother and the offspring" (Rules 6.13) and the risks covers ectopic pregnancy, multiple gestation, spontaneous abortion and Ovarian Hyper Stimulation Syndrome (OHSS) but what is the parameter which will determine which is a small risk and which is a life threatening one. All those risks explained by the ICMR can take the life of a woman but it has categorized those risks as 'small risk' and the bill also remain silent about the serious implications entailed by these risks. By making only the 'married' or 'unmarried' heterosexual couples eligible for the ART, the bill reinforces the patriarchal idea that heterosexuality is the 'norm'. 'In fact, "couple" has defined in such a way in the bill that homosexual couples from other countries (where same sex relations are legal) can avail ART services from India, but not Indian homosexuals' (SAMA, 2009).

Though the Assisted Reproductive Technologies (Regulation) Bill and Rules 2008 is expected to be regulatory in nature as its name defined it as such but in reality the bill has failed to do so. It cannot provide adequate protection to women's health and well being as well as legal remedies to users of ART. 'Through various clauses it tends to promote the interests of the private sector providers of these technologies rather than regulate them' (SAMA, 2009).

Conclusion

Though ART has been criticized on many grounds, it also acts as a liberating force for many women. If we consider ART as liberating for most women, then it liberates only certain group of people in the society especially the high class who can afford this. There is no denying of the fact that technological development in the area of reproduction has helped women to exercise their own agency by enabling them to become mothers. Choose to remain childless is also a reproductive choice but this choice get devalued over the social construction of womanhood. These reproductive technologies have strengthens the patriarchal ideologies rather than addressing it. 'The option of selecting the sex of the child becomes possible and being difficult one-time pregnancies it is nobody's guess what the preferred sex of the child in such pregnancies would be. With a horrendous history of female infanticide and repeated incidences of sex selective abortion in India, ART can make overcoming such social malice even more difficult' (Sahin, 2016). 'The focus for the Indian woman in a patriarchal context is not so much the experience of pregnancy or childbirth but the enormous social pressure and the feeling of security she gets as a result of having a child, especially a male child' (Widge, 2002).

ART has lead to the exploitation of women and makes them more vulnerable than before. Exploitation of women will continue to happen without a stronger regulatory mechanism. Practices which make one section of the humanity more vulnerable need to come under critical observation.

Bibliography

- Agigian, A. (2007). Stratified Reproduction. In G. Ritzer, Blackwell Encyclopedia of Sociology (pp. 4835-4837). Oxford: Blackwell Publishing.
- Annandale, E. 2009. Women's health and social change. New York: Routledge.
- Corea, G. (1985). The Mother Machine: Reproductive Technologies from Artificial Insemination to Artificial Wombs. New York: Harper & Row.
- Marwah, V. & Sarojini N.(2011). Reinventing Reproduction, Re-conceiving Challenges: An Examination of Assisted Reproductive Technologies in India. Economic & political Weekly. Vol. XLVI No. 43.
- Sahin, S. (2016). Assisted Reproductive Technologies and Its Gender Implications with Special Reference to the Middle Class in Guwahati, Assam. IOSR –JHSS, Vol. 21, Issue 6, pp. 21-28.
- SAMA. (2009). Assisted Reproductive Technologies: For whose Benefit? Economic & Political Weekly, Vol. XLIV (no 18).
- Strickler, J. (1992). The new reproductive technology: problem or solution? Sociology of Health & Illness. Vol. 14.

15

Prevalence of Insomnia: A Cross Sectional Study

— ***Mariachristina B, Anbu N***

Abstract

BACKGROUND: *Insomnia, the most common sleep disorder, thus affecting quality of life. It has one or more of the following conditions: difficulty in falling asleep, frequent waking up during the night, waking up too early in the morning.* ***OBJECTIVE:*** *This study was conducted to determine the prevalence of insomnia and to find out various associated factors.* ***METHODOLOGY:*** *An institution based descriptive cross-sectional study was conducted at Aringar Anna Government Hospital of Indian Medicine, by face to face interview according to Athens Insomnia Scale by consecutive sampling, on a sample of 200 participants. Statistical analysis was done by SPSS version 26. Percentage, Chi-square test and logistic regression were used in final analysis.* ***RESULT:*** *About 37.5% of the study population suffered from insomnia as per AIS Score. This study found a significant association of insomnia with gender, BMI, and nocturia.* ***CONCLUSION:*** *This study found difficulty in sleep induction, frequent midnight awakening and day-time sleepiness were the major complaints. Further community based studies are recommended to investigate the magnitude and determinants of this health problem and other life style factors.* ***KEYWORDS:*** *Insomnia, Prevalence, Athens insomnia scale.*

Background

We spend almost one third of our life for sleeping. A quality sleep is essential for good health and well-being. However, lifestyle and environmental factors are causing difficulties in sleeping. Several indicators can be used to describe sleep disorders. These indicators are: (1) Sleep latency (2) Number and duration of nocturnal awakenings (3) The total sleep time (4) Rapid Eye Movement sleep (REM sleep), together with modifications in the autonomic functions (heart-rate, blood pressure, vasoconstriction and respiratory rate); (5) Repetitive nights of sleep disruption among one week or one month.

Insomnia is defined (DSM-5) as difficulty in getting to sleep, staying asleep or having non-restorative sleep despite having adequate opportunity for sleep, together with associated impairment of daytime functioning, with symptoms being present for at least 4 weeks. However, the insomnia is clinically relevant if the patient, presents with insomnia in combination with daytime dysfunction or distress such as fatigue, poor concentration and irritability.

Worldwide epidemiological studies assessed the prevalence of insomnia without restrictive criteria as 33% in general population. When frequency was used to determine the presence of insomnia around countries, it was 17%-34%.Using severity it was 18% and symptoms with daytime consequence was around 16%.Thus overall globally different studies revealed that between 10% to 30% of adults have insomnia at any given point in time and up to 50% -60% have insomnia in a given year.

Most sleep expert agree that the adult sleep requirement is typically between 6 and 10 hours of sleep per 24-hour period with the majority of individuals requiring approximately 8 hours of sleep per day. The tolerated minimum sleep time is approximately 6 hours.

People with insomnia are likely to experience more anxiety and depression, are at more than double the risk of congestive heart failure, hypertension and diabetes, and have an elevated risk of death. Left untreated, insomnia increases the risk of developing other illnesses. Therefore, much more needs to be done to identify and treat insomnia early. This study was conducted to find out the prevalence of insomnia and its associated factors among adult population attending the OPD at Aringar Anna Government Hospital of Indian Medicine.

Methodology

Due permission was sought from the Institutional Ethical Committee at Government Siddha Medical College, Chennai, before the conduct of study. An Institution based observational descriptive study, cross-sectional in design was carried out for 3 months at Aringar Anna Government Hospital of Indian Medicine (OPD), Chennai. The age in between 18 to 60 years were included in this study whereas pregnant ladies and who are not given consent were excluded.

STUDY TOOL: A predesigned, semi structured interview proforma was used to obtain data. The proforma has three sections: **Section A** was used to collect the data related to the socio-demographic variables like age, sex, occupation, marital status. **Section B** was to assess insomnia by a validated Athens Insomnia Scales (AIS) based on ICD-10 criteria. It is measured by assessing 8 factors out of which the first 5 are related to nocturnal sleep and the last 3 related to day time dysfunction. A cut off score e" 6 on the AIS is used to establish the diagnosis of insomnia. **Section C** was used to collect the data related to associated factors of insomnia like environmental issues, snore, medical illness, method to help asleep etc.

SAMPLING TECHNIQUE: Data was collected on sample size 200 by Consecutive sampling among persons accompanying patients attending to the OPD at Aringar Anna Government Hospital of Indian Medicine, Chennai.

METHOD OF DATA COLLECTION: Apparently healthy subjects accompanying patients to this hospital were requested to participate. The purpose as well as the nature of the study was explained to the study participants and they were ensured about their anonymity and confidentiality. Informed consent was taken followed by data collection by face to face interview method. At last any queries that they had were answered.

STATISTICAL ANALYSIS: Data entered in Microsoft office excel and analysis was done by SPSS version 26. Percentage, Chi-square test and logistic regression were used in final analysis.

Result

In this study, the overall prevalence of Insomnia was 37.5% with a female preponderance (29.5%). Out of the total 200 participants, around 69.5% were older than 40 years of age, 71% were females, Majority of the females were house wife (47.5%), and about 89% were married. Majority of the study participants belong to normal BMI (51.5%), and 38.5% were Overweight.

Table (15.1) shows the association of insomnia with different socio-demographic variables. Logistic regression was applied to calculate the unadjusted odds of developing insomnia. We found a statistically significant association of insomnia for gender (90%) and BMI.

Table (15.2) shows the distribution of sleep related symptoms based on Athens Insomnia Scales. We found that the difficulty in sleep induction (55.5%), frequent midnight awakening (56%) and sleepiness during daytime (49.5%) were more common symptoms observed in this study.

Table (15.3) and (15.4) shows associated factors of insomnia and Medical condition that disrupts sleep. We found a statistically significant association of insomnia for method to help asleep (none-85%), bothering of sleep problem (none-43.5% & little bit-30.5%), and nocturia (14.5%).

Table 15.1: Association of socio-demographic variables with Insomnia

Variables	*Insomnia Present (n=75) (%)*	*Insomnia Absent (n=125) (%)*	*Total (n=200) (%)*	*P-value*
Age Group				
20-39	20(10)	41(20.5)	61(30.5)	0.362
40-60	55(27.5)	84(42)	139(69.5)	
Gender				
Male	16(8)	42(21)	58(29)	0.064
Female	59(29.5)	83(41.5)	142(71)	
Occupation				
House Wife	41(20.5)	54(27)	95(47.5)	0.181
Business	4(2)	11(5.5)	15(7.5)	
Self-Employee	22(11)	45(22.5)	67(30.5)	
Engineer	6(3)	5(2.5)	11(5.5)	
Student	2(1)	10(5)	12(6)	
Marital status				
Married	65(32.5)	113(56.5)	178(89)	0.166
Unmarried	7(3.5)	12(6)	19(9.5)	
Divorced	2(1)	0(0)	2(1)	
Widow	1(0.5)	0(0)	1(0.5)	
BMI Group				
Normal	29(14.5)	74(37)	103(51.5)	0.016
Overweight	35(17.5)	42(21)	77(38.5)	
Obese	8(4)	6(3)	14(7)	

Table 15.2: Distribution of sleep related symptoms based on Athens Insomnia Scales:

AIS	*Present*	*Absent*
Sleep Induction	111(55.5)	89(44.5)
Midnight Awakening	112(56)	88(44)
Final Awakening	101(50.5)	99(49.5)
Sleep Duration	124(62)	76(38)
Sleep Quality	104(52)	96(48)
Sense of well Being during the day	72(36)	128(64)
Functioning during the day	100(50)	100(50)
Daytime Sleepiness	99(49.5)	101(50.5)

Table 15.3: Medical condition that disrupts sleep

Sleep apnea	*Insomnia*		*Total*	*P-Value*
	Insomnia Absent	*Insomnia Present*		
Yes	4	2	6	0.831
No	121	73	194	
Total	125	75	200	
chronic pain				
Yes	9	7	16	0.59
No	116	68	184	
Total	125	75	200	
Depression				
Yes	1	2	3	0.293
No	124	73	197	
Total	125	75	200	
GERD				
Yes	5	4	9	0.66
No	120	71	191	
Total	125	75	200	
Nocturia				
Yes	11	18	29	0.003
No	114	57	171	
Total	125	75	200	

Table 15.4: Associated factors of insomnia.

Variables	*Insomnia Present (n=75) (%)*	*Insomnia Absent (n=125) (%)*	*Total (200)*	*P-value*
Can't fall back asleep				
Stay In Bed	37(18.5)	90(45)	127	0.465
Watch TV	21(10.5)	12(6)	33	
Work	17(8.5)	23(11.5)	40	
Environmental issues				
Light Exposure	26(13)	40(20)	66	0.489
Noise	40(20)	62(31)	102	
None	9(4.5)	23(11.5)	32	
Snore				
Yes	29(14.5)	36(18)	65	0.149
No	46(23)	89(44.5)	135	
Any medication				
Diabetes	14(25.9)	14(25.9)	28	0.465
Hypertension	8(14.8)	13(24.1)	21	
Thyroid	1(1.9)	3(5.6)	4	
Kidney Disease	1(1.9)	0(0)	1	

(*Contd...*)

Method to help sleep induction				
None	57(28.5)	113(56.5)	170	0.023
Medication	12(6)	4(2)	16	
Food Habits	4(2)	4(2)	8	
Alcohol	1(0.5)	2(1)	3	
Yoga/Meditation	1(0.5)	2(1)	3	
Sleep problem				
None	3(1.5)	84(42)	87	<0.001**
Little Bit	20(10)	41(20.5)	61	
Moderate	38(19)	0()	38	
Extreme	14(7)	0()	14	

Discussion

This study has found prevalence of insomnia as 37.5% in apparently healthy South Indian population above 18 years of age which is less than the reported prevalence of 18% by Panda et al who had used the Epworth Sleepiness Scale and Pitts-burg Sleep Quality Index for assessing insomnia. We chose Athens Insomnia Scale because it is simple and easy to understand. A prevalence of 13.3% was reported in studies by Sanjeev Kumar, Amrita Kumari respectively, among patients using same scale as used in this study.

Insomnia was found significantly higher in age group above 40 years (90%), which is consistent with other similar studies although, this was not-shown in all the studies. Similarly whereas the female preponderance of insomnia is corroborated by other studies as well (29.5%).

Married persons tended to be at higher risk of suffering from Insomnia contrary to the inference of a review study. This could be due to higher number of married persons (32.5%) in the sample. Occupation did not show any significant association as mentioned in a review article.

Insomnia was found statistically significant with method to help asleep (none-28.5%- out of 75), most of the patients did not take any method for sleep induction, and also nocturia (14.5%) was found significantly associate with Insomnia. Several other studies have also reported that nocturia is associated with disrupted sleep.

Environmental issues, snore, medication did not show any significant with Insomnia. Difficulty in sleep initiation (55.5%), frequent midnight awakenings (56%) and day time sleepiness (49.5%) were the major complaints by the respondents.

Conclusion

There is a high prevalence of insomnia 37.5% among adult population aged between 18 to 60 years attending Out Patient Department at Arignar Anna Government Hospital of Indian Medicine, Chennai. Females are more prone (29.5%) to insomnia than males. In spite of that, most of them did not seek any medical help (85%) for their condition. Hence, it is an under reported problem. This study found a significant relationship of insomnia with gender, BMI, Method to help asleep, and nocturia. Associated factors such as environmental issues, snore, medication did not show any significant with insomnia. Difficulty in sleep induction (55.5%), frequent midnight awakenings (56%) and day-time sleepiness (49.5%) were the major complaints. Further community-based studies are recommended to investigate the magnitude and determinants of this health problem and other life style factors.

Limitations of the Study

As this study was conducted on healthy persons, who were patients' attendants at Aringar Anna Government Hospital of Indian Medicine, Chennai, the results cannot be generalized to the whole population. Another limitation of this study is that we did not classify insomnia into primary and secondary. Associated factors were not measured in detail.

Bibilography

- WHO technical meeting on sleep and health, WHO, Europe, 2004.
- Kumari R, Gupta RK, Langer B, Singh P, Akhtar N, Anuradha. Insomnia and its associated factors: A cross-sectional study in rural adults of North India. Int J Med Sci Public Health 2018; 7(10): 800-804.
- Clinical practice guideline Adult insomnia: Assessment to diagnosis, 2007.
- Mausumi Basu, Sita Chatterjee, Abhishek De, Debasish Sinha, Afifa Ahamed, Raghunath; A Study on Prevalence of Chronic Insomnia and it's Association with Medical Co morbidities; 2017.
- Hassan Abdullah Shakeel, Hamza Maqsood, Asher Ishaq, Basit Ali, Humza Hussain, Aliraz Khan, Syed Asfand Yar Shah; Insomnia among medical students: across-section alstudy; 2019.
- Panda S, Taly AB, Sinha S, Gururaj G, Girish N, Nagaraja D. Sleep related disorder among a healthy population in South India, 2012.
- Kumar A, Kumari B, Manasa RV, Das SC, Ghoshal V. Insomnia among attendants of patients in a tertiary care hospital at Visakhapatnam, 2018.

16

A Study on Solar Cooker and Its Impact on Women Health in India

— ***Dr. D. Swamikannan,***
N. Periyamayan

Abstract

Energy plays a crucial role in human activity, economic and community development of a nation. The use of energy in a home has a considerable effect on the environment, people health and longevity of women. In many developing countries in the world, people are using solid fuels, biomass, kerosene, coal, and diesel for their basic needs such as cooking, heating, etc. These sources are limited, inefficient, environmentally polluted sources. If these resources are continuously used it may cause for indoor and outdoor air pollution and produce different types of illness such as asthma, cataracts, tuberculosis etc, these diseases which seriously affects women than that of men. The World Health Organization reported that 60 per cent of premature deaths is from household air pollution happening in women and children in the world. Further, the using of biomass women are faced several problems such as more time spent to collect the fuel collection, increased the burden of cleaning utensils, walls, floors, and clothes. As a result, they are unable to do income-generating activities and the concentration of maintaining their health is low. Of the total demand of Liquefied Petroleum Gas (LPG), 75 per cent is imported from the foreign countries which required more foreign money. The objective of the study is to know the off grid-connected device of solar cookers in India and examine solar cooker and its impact on women health in India. The methodology of the study is based on a secondary source of information. The finding of the study shows that India's installation of the solar cooker has been declined and remaining constant during the period of the study. The solar cooker is the clean, healthy, non-polluted and eco-friendly system. It is technically and commercially viable option for pollution-free cooking, especially in areas with abundant solar radiation. The solar cooking system provides a positive method of deploying solar energy for meeting considerable cooking energy and also save the natural source.

Keywords: *Solar cooker, Eco-friendly, Women, Foreign exchange.*

Introduction

Energy plays a crucial role in human activity, economic and social development of a nation. The usage of energy in a household has a considerable effect on the environment, for the health of family members, and the lives of women. However, in majority of the developing countries in the world, people are using the solid fuels, biomass (fuelwood, dung and crop residues), kerosene, coal, and diesel for their cooking needs (ESMAP, 2004). World Energy Outlook Report (2017) reveals that household air pollution is mostly affected by women and children across the world. Almost 3.1 billion people are still depending upon the polluting, inefficient energy systems, for their heating and lighting purposes in the world. It is the most inefficient form of a cooking system, which leads to harmful to human health and the environment.

Further, the burning of conventional sources is releasing smokes, which expose carbon dioxide (CO2) that leads to pollution. Of which, indoor and outdoor air pollutions are producing different types of disease such as asthma, cataracts, tuberculosis, adverse pregnancy outcomes, in particular, low birth weight, ischaemic heart disease, interstitial lung disease, nasopharyngeal and laryngeal cancers (WHO, 2006). Around 3.8 million of the premature deaths household air occurs in the world. Women experience higher individual exposure levels than men, due to their greater involvement in daily cooking and other domestic activities. The single biggest killer of children aged less than five years worldwide is pneumonia (WHO, 2016).

Women play a vital role in the cooking system in India. However, in India, 819 million people still use traditional biomass cooking stoves for their cooking needs as well as 1 million premature deaths due to household air pollution occurs every year by using the biomass-based cooking stoves (CEEW report, 2017). Most of the people in India are living in rural areas. The people are mostly preferred to use fuelwood because they are economically very poor therefore they are unable to buy the clean cooking system. Besides, the availability of firewood is easily accessible and economically viable for these people. For this reason, most of their time is spending to fuelwood collections which are an additional burden to the women (Das et al. 2019). Therefore, they do not time spend to the income generation activities, maintaining the health conditions. In this circumstance, need to change the alternative cooking system, it is based on the healthy, non-polluted, renewable and eco-friendly system.

Solar power is a promising solution to conventional sources. It contributes a major role in human development and economic growth of the country. At presently, the utilization of solar energy is increased and the price of the solar panel is gradually decreased around the world. Further, the majorities of the countries are adopted solar energy policy for promoting environmental protection and accomplish sustainable development goals. Among the cooking systems in renewable energies, the solar cooking system is technically and commercially viable option for pollution-free cooking, especially in areas with abundant solar radiation. The solar cooking system provides a positive method of deploying solar energy for meeting considerable cooking energy and also save the natural source.

Statement of the Problem

The use of traditional cooking stoves and fossil fuels pose a serious threat to human health and environment, especially to women's health. According to the Council on Energy, Environment and Water report, in India, 50 per cent of the households are depending on traditional biomass for their cooking, and heating requires. Uses of conventional source for their cooking needs makes women encounter several problems such as more time spent to collect the fuelwood collection, increased the workload of cleaning utensils, walls, floors, and clothes, which negatively affect their health. Among the spending time women spend much more time on unpaid work as compared to men because their cooking activities thereby using the inefficient cooking system of the traditional cooking system. It is complexity to sight and breathing over long time women and children (CEEW report, 2017).

The household solid fuels burning are the major way of creating disease women. According to the Health Effects Institute report, 267,700 deaths owe from the combustion of residential biomass in India. Of which more deaths incurre on women and children which is a consequence of indoor pollution (HEI, 2018). The Liquid Petroleum Gas (LPG) is one of the fossil fuel sources which is exhausted source as well as the environmentally polluted and nonrenewable source. The fossil fuel source based cooking system expresses CO2 emission, it leads to air pollution, health problems, global warming and climate change whilst which destructs the natural resources. Almost 207 million of households are using the LPG connections around the country. The LPG is a byproduct of natural gas extraction and crude oil refining. The 88 per cent of the households unable to adopt the LPG connection because the cost of LPG connection is very high (CEEW Report, 2017). The government of India provides a lump amount of money to spending on subsidy of LPG connection due to cannot spend the social welfare scheme. Most of the crude oil is imported from other countries as a result of foreign money is losses. However, solar cooking system, solar dryer and solar-powered devices are depending on solar radiation, in the winter and rainy seasons which is not suitable. The price of solar devices are very high and if any compliant or service of the solar device is very complicated to service the device because the limited-service centre is there (Chaudhari et al., 2017).

Objectives of the Study

The present study has two objectives which are listed below.

1. To know the status of the off grid-connected device of the solar cooker in India
2. To examine the impact of the solar cooker on women health in India.

Methodology

The present study is exclusively based on a secondary source of information. This information is collected from the various articles in reputed peer-reviewed journals, magazines, government and nongovernment reports. Further, the data were collected from the Energy Statistics 2018 published by Ministry of Statistics and Programme implementation and Ministry of New and Renewable Energy, Government of India.

Review of Literature

Vijay Laxmi, et.al (2003) study shows that women are facing a lot of hard work owing to the use of biofuels. They are walking to collect the fuelwood was approximately 2.5km and 50 hours per month per household are expended in fuelwood collection and transportation. The use of kerosene for cooking is negligible in the area, because of unavailability more than non-affordability. It is revealed that the health impacts of the use of bio-fuels are quite high for adult women. The linkages between many socio-economic variables and respiratory symptoms in adult women show that health impacts can be reduced by increasing female literacy, reducing the use of bio-fuels, and changing the housing design by, for example, introducing ventilation or separating the kitchen from the living area. The losses incurred because of cooking fuels, including workdays, spent expenditure on illness and lost working days due to illness are Rs. 29 billion per year in the rural areas of Rajasthan.

Sengar et al (2010) study reveal that the temperature profiles of the developed solar cooker are slightly better than the commercially available fibre body of solar cooker. It is found that low-cost solar cooker is 0.122 and 0.55 which are higher as compared to the commercial solar cooker values of 0.115 and 0.43. It's payback period showed that the developed solar cooker concerning a variety of fuels such as firewood, kerosene, LPG, coal, and electricity are in the range of three months to less than two years.

Kimambo (2007) study shows that the most of the cookers could be used to cook food for households in areas with medium and high insolation, with appropriate selection of the type and specification of the cookers. The specification should be based on the measured insolation data of the location indication of the direct and diffuse components. Further, the study reveals that as a guiding tool, reflector cookers offer best comparative performance in areas with longest durations of clear sky, panel and collector cookers under moderate cloudy conditions and box cookers under very cloudy conditions.

Mendoza et al (2019) study indicates that the home-made solar cooker is to enhance the standard of living of the society. It is revealed that the using of solar cooker is annually reduced by 42.6kt and 4.2 kt greenhouse gas emissions and waste generation respectively. Additionally, 67GWh of electricity and €23.2 million can be saved by each year. Solar cooker leads to the sustainable development of the country.

Scenario of Solar power in India

Solar energy is one of the renewable energy sources on earth. It is the clean, unexhausted and environmentally friendly source. Solar power provides a huge amount of energy with negligible emissions of greenhouse gases. India is gifted with greater solar energy resource due to its geographical structure in the equatorial Sun Belt of the earth, and having around 300 sunny days in a year. The theoretically calculated solar energy incidence on its land area alone is about 5000 trillion kilowatt-hours (kWh) per year (Rathore, 2017). India's total renewable energie potential is 1095MW of which wind power potential is more than 300 GW at a hub height of 100 metre and solar power potential is 750GW which is assumed. Further, the potential of small hydropower is 20 GW and Bio-energy potential is 25 GW in India. Among the renewable energies in India, solar power potential is very high as compared to other renewable energies.

India has launched the world's largest renewable energy programme in January 2010. The National Solar Mission (NSM) was the first mission to be operated under the National Action Plan on Climate change (NAPCC). Using a three-phase approach, the mission's objective is to establish India as a global leader in solar energy, by creating the policy conditions for solar technology diffusion across the country as quickly as possible. The initial target of the mission of installing 20 GW grid-connected solar power plants by the year 2022 was improved to 100 GW to be achieved by the same target year. According to the Ministry of New and Renewable Energy annual report, India is achieved the 5th place for deploying the solar power across the world. Further, more than 10 million man day's employment is being created in the sector. Solar power capacity is increased by more than 11 times in the last five years from 2.6 GW to 28.18 GW in March 2019 (MNRE Annual report, 2018-2019).

Status of Solar Cooker in India

Solar cooking is an emerging device in developing countries like India. It is the simplest, safest, clean, eco-friendly and most suitable way to cook food without consuming conventional sources or heating the kitchen. It is a device that cooks food using only solar energy in the form of solar radiation (Rajendra et al, 2012). This is not a new idea which also recognized in the 19th century. The potential of the sun's energy is to offer heat for cooking and other purposes and designed proper tools to harness it. The solar cooker is to provide more benefits to their stakeholder and the environment. To reduce the health risks, fossil fuels consumption and reduce the environmental contamination thereby to get economic benefits and conserve the environment (Aadiwal et.al, 2017). It uses the energy of direct sunlight to heat, cook or food or drink. The solar cooker is generally used in some situations such as where the least fuel consumption, the danger of accidental fires is high and considering the health and ecological consequences and also which is no fuel and no cost for operating. The solar cooker can be easily dismantled and assembled by anybody and thus may be satisfactorily packed and transported anywhere in the country (Energetica India, 2014). Here, there are many designs available such as solar panel cooker, solar parabolic cooker, solar box type cooker and hybrid solar cooker etc. At, presently, the development of Photovoltaic a thermal hybrid solar cooker has started a new horizon in the field of solar cookers as the cooking is faster than conventional box type. Besides, the solar cooker can be used at the user's convenient time. The cooker was converted into the solar dryer by small modification and can be used for drying vegetables. It is also commercially available in the market (Joshi and Thakkar, 2017). Solar cookers have some salient features as followed by community cooking, indoor cooking, fast cooking, cooking of traditional food, automatic tracking, seasonal adjustment and multiple users.

Community cooking: It is possible to cook for 40 to 50 persons with 7 square meter dish cooker. One dish cooker may take 1-2 hours which is depending on the type of dish and solar insolation available. Almost, majority of the places are receiving enough insolation of solar energy. Therefore it is possible to cook two meals with the cooker in those areas.

Indoor Cooking: The solar rays are directed into the kitchen, which enables cooking indoors. The cook, therefore, does not have to go outside in the sun to load and unload the cooking pots as being done in Box Solar Cooker.

Fast Cooking: Solar cooker quickly does the cooking work due to the high temperature and power at the focal point.

The cooking of Traditional Food

It also possible to cook almost all traditional dishes including chapattis, purees, dosha, etc.

Automatic Tracking: There is an automatic clockwork arrangement which rotates the outside primary reflector to track the sun routinely. It has to set this reflector in focus only once a day in the morning and thereafter for the rest of the time the clockwork keeps on rotating the reflector automatically.

Multiple Uses: Solar cooker is not only used for cooking which is also used in hot water production (Energetica India, 2014).

Results and Discussion

The solar cooker is deployed in many places such as residential schools, institutional kitchens, industrial and administrative canteens, religious ashrams, hotels, hospitals, police and armed forces kitchens, etc. One solar cooker can serve to 50 peoples and 35-45 LPG cylinders can be saved in per year (https://mnre.gov.in). Solar energy is can ensure replacement of polluting biomass/ imported LPG with the cheaper and green source of energy. India has taken an initiative to replace biomass/LPG with solar PV cooking system. So far, two pilot projects completed in solar PV cooking system. The 173 solar cookstoves are provided in two villages, of which 74 cookstoves are provided in Bancha Village, Betul district of Madhya Pradesh and 99 cookstoves provided at Chouldari Tsunami shelters, South Andaman in India (MNRE, 2018-19). In 2002, world largest solar cooker was installed at Tirupati Devasthanam, Andhra Pradesh in India. The system is put up at the Nitya Annadanam complex at Tirumala can prepare food for 15,000 persons at a time. Nearly 50,000 kg of rice along with sambar and rasam are cooked in the kitchens of Tirumala every day of the year without using conventional sources (Akshya Urja, 2011).

Table 1: Installation of off-grid Device of Solar Cooker in India

Year	*Solar cookers (Nos)*
2009-2010	663501
2010-2011	663501
2011-2012	1221
2012-2013	1221
2013-2014	1221
2014-2015	1221
Total	**1331886**

Source: Ministry of New and Renewable Energy: Energy Statistics 2013, Central Statistics Office.

Above the table 1 shows that the total installation of solar cookers is 1,331886. Besides, installation trend is declining from 2009 to 2015.

Role of Solar Cooker and Its Impact on Women Health in India

Cooking is an unavoidable daily activity in the household which requires a huge amount of energy and human effort. In developing countries, the majority of the population is residing in a rural area they are mostly used in biomass. According to World Health Organization, among the solid fuel use regions in the world, South East Asian region is the second-largest user in solid fuels which is accounted by 63 per cent in 2013 in the world. It shows that 3 million people are still relying on solid fuels, kerosene in open fires and inefficient stoves for their cooking needs. They are economically very poor and mostly live in middle income and low-income countries. This context reveals that majority of the people are still depending upon these kinds of sources In India, 500 million of people are still use in solid biomass for their primary cooking fuel (WHO, 2016, DNAP, 2017). It poses serious trouble to human being and the environment. The combustion of these sources is created several problems such as pollution, deforestation, Co2 emission, diseases, climate change, global warming which are leads to an unfavourable impact on human health and environment (Chakra borty, et al, 2014).

The solar cooking system could solve these problems. It is clean because which do not generate smoke as the conventional use of firewood for cooking. As well, the solar cooker is a renewable, non-polluted, eco-friendly and safety source it can reduce the use of solid firewood in low and middle-income countries. The solar cooker can produce yearly thermal energy of around 317.63 kWh which heat power is enough to cook the food solar cooking device is the best system for both household and institutional type of cooking system and it leads to attaining the sustainable development goals (Otte, 2014).

The cooking of solid biomass fuel-based energy system generates indoor and outdoor pollutions on the earth. It is very serious problems in the society, which creates different types of diseases incurred on the human being in which mostly affected by women on the back of spending of time is high as compared to the male. If continuously using of biomass cooking system it may create respiratory and eye-related diseases such as asthma, cataracts, tuberculosis eye irritation, shortness of breath, cough and dizziness, etc. Mohapatra et al (2018) indicate that exposure to biomass fuel smoke is significantly associated with the prevalence of symptoms of headache, dry cough, and Hypertension. The household air pollution and health report show that the around 3.8 million (60 per cent) people are deaths in a year from indoor air pollution due to the inefficient use of solid fuels and kerosene for cooking. Among the deaths, 27 per cent of deaths are caused by pneumonia, 27 per cent of deaths from ischaemic heart disease, 18 per cent from stroke, 20 per cent of deaths from chronic obstructive pulmonary disease and 8 per cent deaths from lung cancer in the world (Household air pollution and Health, 2018).

The producing of both indoor and outdoor pollution's basic reason is the emission of greenhouse gas which was mostly came from the burning of firewood and the use of conventional sources. Besides, the harvest of wood for cooking leads to deforestation, negative impact on wild animals' eco-system and reducing the carbon uptake by forests. The solar cooker can reduce the consumption of 127.05 kg of wood which corresponds to 123.87 kg of CO2 emission per year. In the interior areas like a desert, even the wood is not available. The solar cooker can boiling temperature of the water for disinfection purposes, which is enough to kill pathogenic bacteria, viruses and parasites and the suitable energy required for obtaining well consumable food (Riahi et al., 2018).

Additionally, women are confronted with several problems such as fuel collection, increased burden of cleaning utensils, walls, floors, and clothes, ecological changes and so on are negative externalities. The solid biomass fuel based cookstove and practice is required 5-8 hours on per day about cooking activities whereas the using of firewood are frequently exhausted and the process of collecting firewood is needed 20 per cent of the time in per day (Clean Alliance for clean cookstoves report, 2013). As a result, they are unable to do income-generating activities and the concentration of maintaining their health is low (Laxmi et al, 2003).

The solar cooker requires very little maintenance and reduced the more time of cooking, collection of firewood and save the natural resource. If adopting the solar cooker they are easily and quickly finish the cooking activities and remaining times they can involve income generative activities thereby women are empowered and enhance their quality of life. In the institutional large scale, solar cooking is (hotel, restaurant, school, college hostel etc) save a large number of fossil fuels, and reduces the environmental consequences (Renuka Prasad et al, 2017).

Presently, Liquefied Petroleum Gas (LPG) is a most well-liked cooking fuel in India. It is a fossil fuel source of energy and is a limited and unsustainable source. Also, it is produced from crude oil, which is mostly imported (75 Per cent) from the foreign countries for this reason the country is losing the much more amount of foreign money. Hence, it is an indirect adverse impact on the country's economy, human health and environmental damage. Solar energy is the plentiful source, unlimited supply and which is sufficient to fulfil the present energy demand and future energy demand of the world.

Conclusion

Cooking is an exercise which is performed in each of the households for at least two times a day. The fossil fuel and traditional cooking system is exposing the different type of health problems incurred on human being and environment and also these which are low efficient. Solar energy based cooking system is found to the best alternative for cooking. In India, most of the states are receiving much more sun's radiations per year. The concluding of the study is the installation solar cooker trend is declining and total installation of solar cookers is 1,331886 from 2009 to 2015. The solar cooker is the best option for cooking because of their insignificant maintenance cost and subsidies on capital cost are provided by the government of India. Its operating time is very low and does not create smoke, as well as which is reduced the Co2 emission, deforestation, pollutions, health problems, and environmentally friendly. Therefore, the solar cooking system offers a positive method of deploying solar energy for meeting considerable cooking energy and also save the natural source.

References

- Joint UNDP/World Bank Energy Sector Management Assistance Programme Report (2004), "The Impact of Energy on Women's Lives in Rural India report" published by The International Bank for Reconstruction and Development, The World Bank 1818 H Street, N.W. Washington, D.C. 20433, U.S.A.
- Energy Access Outlook: from Poverty to Prosperity, World Energy Outlook 2017 Special Report, Published by International Energy Agency, France.
- "Fuel for Life Household Energy and Health Report" (2006), Published by World Health Organization, pp. 1-34
- World Health Organization Report (2016), "Burning Opportunity: Clean Household Energy for Health, Sustainable Development, and Wellbeing of Women and Children" pp. 1-113.
- Sasmita Patnaik, Saurabh Tripathi (2017) "Access to Clean Cooking Energy in India State of the Sector" Published by Council on Energy, Environment & Water Report, Thapar House, 124, Janpath, New Delhi 110001, India pp. 1-24.
- Karabee Das, Greeshma Pradhan, and Sanderine Nonhebel, "Human Energy and Time Spent by Women Using Cooking Energy Systems: A Case Study of Nepal", Energy, Vol. 182, 2019, pp. 493-501.
- Sasmita Patnaik, Saurabh Tripathi (2017) "Access to Clean Cooking Energy in India State of the Sector" Published by Council on Energy, Environment & Water Report, Thapar House, 124, Janpath, New Delhi 110001, India pp. 1-24.
- GBD MAPS Working Group (2018), "Burden of Disease Attributable to Major Air Pollution Sources in India Special Report", 21. Boston, MA: Health Effects Institute.
- Sasmita Patnaik, Saurabh Tripathi (2017) "Access to Clean Cooking Energy in India State of the Sector" Published by Council on Energy, Environment & Water Report, Thapar House, 124, Janpath, New Delhi 110001, India pp. 1-24.
- Vijay Laxmi, Jyoti Parikh, Shyam Karmakar and Pramod Dabrase, "Household Energy, Women's Hardship and Health Impacts in Rural Rajasthan, India: Need for Sustainable Energy Solutions", Energy for Sustainable Development, Vol. 7 (1), March 2003, pp. 50-68.

- Namrata Sengar, Prabha Dashora and Sunita Mahavar, "Low Cost Solar Cooker: Promising Solution towards Reducing Indoor Air Pollution from Solid Fuel Use", Indian Journal of Science and Technology, Vol. 3 (10), 2010, pp. 1038-1042.
- C Z M Kimambo, "Development and Performance Testing of Solar Cookers", Journal of Energy in Southern Africa, Vol. 18 (3), 2007, pp. 41-51.
- Joan Manuel F. Mendoza, Alejandro Gallego-Schmid, Ximena C. Schmidt Rivera, Joan Rieradevall, and Adisa Azapagic, "Sustainability Assessment of Home-Made Solar Cookers for Use in Developed Countries", Science of the Total Environment, Vol. 648 (2019), pp. 184–196.
- Pushpendra Kumar Singh Rathore, Shailendra Rathore, and Rudra Pratap Singh Sugandha Agnihotri, "Solar Power Utility Sector in India: Challenges and Opportunities", Renewable and Sustainable Energy Reviews, 2017, pp. 1-17.
- Annual Report 2018-2019, Published by Ministry of New and Renewable Energy, Government of India.
- Rajendra C. Patil Mahesh M. Rathore and Manojkumar Chopra, "An Overview of Solar Cookers", Special Issue of International Journal of electronics, Communication & Soft Computing Science & Engineering, March 2012, pp. 258-264.
- Rahul Aadiwal, Manish Hassani, and Pradeep Kumar, "An Overview Study of Solar Cookers", International Research Journal of Engineering and Technology, Vol. 4(10), 2017, pp. 1651-1655.
- http://www.energeticaindia.net/download.php?seccion=articles&archivo=2 7vsCM5wUN89ijn VUkKPWOQldwoccOLSK7NH50cG7Zof BzmJE0YUj.pdf.
- Smita B Joshi, and Hemant Thakkar, "Solar Cooker- A Review", Solar Cooker International, 6th SCI World Conference, 2017, At: Muni Seva Ashram, Goraj, dist. Vadodara, Gujarat, India.
- https://mnre.gov.in/file-manager/UserFiles/Brief_Indoor_Community_Solar_Cookers.pdf
- Annual Report 2018-2019, Published by Ministry of New and Renewable Energy, Government of India.
- Akshay Urja, "The Success Story, Tirupati the Green Temple" Vol. 4(5), April 2011, p. 44.
- Ministry of New and Renewable Energy: Energy Statistics 2013, Central statistics office.
- World Health Organization Report (2016), "Burning Opportunity: Clean Household Energy for Health, Sustainable Development, and Wellbeing of Women and Children" pp. 1-113.
- Draft National Energy Policy NITI Aayog, Government of India Version as on 27.06.2017.

- Deep Chakraborty, Naba Kumar Mondal, Jayanta Kumar Datta, "Indoor pollution from Solid Biomass Fuel and Rural Health Damage: A Micro-Environmental study in Rural area of Burdwan, West Bengal" International Journal of Sustainable Built Environment, Vol. 3 (2014) pp. 262–271.
- Pia Piroschka Otte (2014), "Warming up To Solar Cooking- a Comparative Study On Motivations and The Adoption Of Institutional Solar Cookers in Developing Countries", Energy Procedia, Vol. 57, pp. 1632-1641.
- Mohapatra I, Das SC, Samantaray S (2018), Health Impact on Women Using Solid Cooking Fuels in Rural Area of Cuttack district, Odisha. J Family Med Prim Care, Vol. 7, pp. 11-5.
- https://www.who.int/news-room/fact-sheets/detail/household-air-pollution-and-health.
- A. Riahi, A. Ben Haj Ali, A. A. Guizani, M. Balghouthi, "Investigation of Solar Cooker Applications for Rural and Remote Areas", Journal of Materials and Environment Sciences, Vol. 9 (8), pp. 2438-2448.
- https://www.cleancookingalliance.org/binary-data/RESOURCE/file/000/000/204-1.pdf
- Vijay Laxmi, Jyoti Parikh, Shyam Karmakar and Pramod Dabrase (2003), "Household Energy, Women's Hardship and Health Impacts in Rural Rajasthan, India: Need for Sustainable Energy Solutions", Energy for Sustainable Development, Vol. 7 (1), pp. 50-68.
- A. Renuka Prasad, Sumer Singh, Harish Nagar, Importance of Solar Energy Technologies for Development of Rural Area in India", International Journal of Scientific Research in Science and Technology, Vol. 3(6), 2017, pp. 585-599.

17

Effectiveness of Structured Teaching Programme on Knowledge Regarding Management of Self among Primigravida Mothers with Pregnancy Induced Hypertension

— ***Radha***

Abstract

The present study was conducted to evaluate the effectiveness of structured teaching programme on knowledge regarding management of self among primigravida mothers with pregnancy induced hypertension and receiving care at selected hospitals, in Chennai. A quasi experimental research design with one group pretest post test design was adopted for the study. Sixty primigravida mothers attending the antenatal OPD was selected using non probability convenience sampling technique. Data was collected using structured interview schedule for assessing the knowledge of primigravida mothers regarding pregnancy induced hypertension. The data was analyzed using descriptive statistics and inferential statistics like t test and chi – square test. The findings of the study revealed that there was a significant increase in the overall knowledge regarding management of self with pregnancy induced hypertension among primigravida women after the structured teaching programme at $P < 0.05$ level of significance. Hence the study concluded that providing health awareness to the primigravida women was to found to be effective in enhancing the knowledge of the antenatal mothers in creating awareness about the *condition, helps to identify the warning signs of pregnancy induced hypertension by managing themselves and helps them in preventing the complications to the fetus.*

Key words: *Pregnancy induced hypertension, structured teaching programme, management of self, knowledge, primigravida mothers.*

Introduction

Pregnancy is one of the most wonderful and noble services imposed by nature. Most of the women may not have many problems during pregnancy, but the unlucky ones, face problems related to pregnancy and child birth. In developing countries, pregnancy and child birth are some of the leading causes of death for women in reproductive age group. Yet, the fate of these women and children is too often overlooked or ignored. The concept of **"make every mother and child count"** reflects the reality that today, government and the international community needs to make the health of the women and children the top priority.

Pregnancy induced hypertension is ominous; pregnancy specific disease, most often associated with severe maternal complication, is a high risk for the fetus. The incidence of Pregnancy induced hypertension is about 5 – 15 % of all pregnancies. UN Millennium Summit 2006 states that about 12% of maternal death is due to Pregnancy induced hypertension. Though no perfect remedy is available at present, it is possible to minimize these hazards on the mother and the developing fetus by early detection and prompt action.

Most of the complications related to Pregnancy induced hypertension are occurring due to maternal negligence or unawareness of the disease and its management. Management of self offers a real potential for improving their health and thus helps to prevent the severe form of Pregnancy induced hypertension at a reduced health cost. Management of self would be the most effective and appropriate approach to enhance both maternal and fetal well being, as well as the successful outcome of pregnancy. Early identification and education about the warning signs of Pregnancy induced hypertension is important in order to initiate early treatment and to prevent worsening of the disease.

With this background the present study was undertaken to determine the effectiveness of structured teaching programme on the knowledge of primigravida mothers regarding pregnancy induced hypertension.

Objectives

The study sought to (a) to assess the existing knowledge regarding management of self among primigravida mothers with pregnancy induced hypertension and receiving care. (b) to assess the knowledge regarding management of self among primigravida mothers with pregnancy induced hypertension and receiving care, after the structured teaching programme. (c) to compare the pre and post teaching knowledge scores regarding management of self among primigravida mothers with pregnancy induced hypertension and receiving care with selected demographic variables. (d) to associate the knowledge sores regarding management of self among primigravida mothers with pregnancy induced hypertension and receiving care with selected demographic variables.

Review of literature

For the present study the review was done under three headings:

- Review related to pregnancy induced hypertension
- Review related to management of self with pregnancy induced hypertension
- Review relate to the effectiveness of structured teaching programme

Bobak and Jensen (2017) defined pregnancy induced hypertension as the development of hypertension after twenty weeks of gestation in a previously normotensive woman without signs of proteinuria or edema.

Pilliterri (2016) reported that pregnancy induced hypertension tends to occur more frequent in primigravida mothers less than 20 years and above 30 years, in low socio economic status (due to poor nutrition).

Omu A.E et al (1996) conducted a comparative study to find out the association between pregnancy induced hypertension and the maternal mortality and morbidity among 224 pregnant hypertensive and 224 normotensive samples. The study findings concluded that the incidence of pregnancy induced hypertension was 4.9 %.and it leads to more hospitalization, intra uterine growth restriction and more number of operative deliveries than the normotensive controls.

Adle Philliterri (2017) states that regular antenatal care is directed towards the prevention and early detection of pregnancy induced hypertension. Periodic weight checking, monitoring blood pressure, salt restricted diet and detection of edema in the antenatal period helps in the prevention of pregnancy induced hypertension. Good nutrition, sufficient rest and weight control can help to minimize the severity.

Red man & Barbara Kelly (2000) stated that the key principles underpin good midwifery care of every pregnant woman, including a sound knowledge base, meeting the woman's needs and enhancing care. Normal antenatal care with regular measurement of blood pressure remains the mainstay of screening for hypertension in pregnancy. The midwives role is that of accurate assessment and communication of when to detect the warning signs of hypertension.

Jeyalakshmi (2000) conducted a study to assess the effectiveness of the structured teaching programme on the management of discomforts among primigravida and multigravida mothers in Chennai. The samples were sixty antenatal mothers. One group pre and post test with control group design was adopted for the study. The findings of the study concluded that the structured teaching programme was found to be effective in the development of thinking capacity of the antenatal mothers and helps them to take wiser decisions when needed.

Leeners B, Rath W et al (2006) conducted a study to examine the satisfaction report with the medical information provided by their health care providers among 620 mothers with pregnancy induced hypertension. Of them 68.6% of the women were not satisfied by the information provided by the health care personnel. They stated that they should be informed about the disease and its potential complications as early as possible. They also concluded that health counseling is their utmost need during this condition.

Hence it was concluded structured teaching programme by the midwives is very essential for the antenatal mothers with pregnancy induced hypertension.

Materials and methods

The study adopted the conceptual framework based on general systems theory by Von Bertalanffy based on the input, through out and the output model of care. A quantitative evaluative approach was selected for the study. Quasi experimental one group pretest post test design was adopted for the study. Sixty primigravida mothers attending the antenatal OPD were selected using non probability convenience sampling technique.

Criteria for sample selection

Primigravida mothers who are

- with pregnancy induced hypertension who are above 20 and less than 36 weeks of gestation.
- attending the OPD for the second antenatal visit and above.
- can understand Tamil or English.

The selection and development of the tool consists of the following sections

Section A: it consists of questions seeking details of demographic data.

Section B: it consists of structured questionnaires to assess the knowledge regarding the management of self with pregnancy induced hypertension on the following aspects : general information regarding pregnancy induced hypertension and management of self with pregnancy induced hypertension.

The structured teaching programme was developed in the aspects of pregnancy induced hypertension – definition, predisposing factors, signs and symptoms, diagnosis, warning signs, maternal and fetal complications of pregnancy induced hypertension.

The management of self was designed with the aspects of regular antenatal visit, bed rest, dietary intake, regular intake of medications, identification of warning signs and regular follow up.

Results

The study results obtained after conducting the study were discussed under the following headings.

Table 17.1: Pre teaching knowledge scores regarding management of self among primigravida mothers with pregnancy induced hypertension

N=60

Sl. No.	*Knowledge on*	*Level of knowledge*					
		Inadequate		*Moderately adequate*		*Adequate*	
		No	*%*	*No*	*%*	*No*	*%*
1	General information about pregnancy induced hypertension	60	100%	-	-	-	-
2	Management of self with pregnancy induced hypertension	59	99%	1	1%	-	-
	Overall knowledge	60	100%				

Table 17.1 reveals that among 60 samples majority 100% of the mothers had inadequate knowledge regarding management of self with pregnancy induced hypertension.

Table 17.2: Post teaching knowledge scores regarding management of self among primigravida mothers with pregnancy induced hypertension

N=60

Sl. No.	*Knowledge on*	*Level of knowledge*					
		Inadequate		*Moderately adequate*		*Adequate*	
		No	*%*	*No*	*%*	*No*	*%*
1	General information about pregnancy induced hypertension	-	-	17	28%	43	72%
2	Management of self with pregnancy induced hypertension	-	-	16	27%	44	74%
	Overall knowledge	-	-	13	22%	47	78%

Table 17.2 reveals that among 60 samples majority 78% of the mothers had adequate knowledge and 22 % of the mothers had moderately adequate knowledge regarding management of self with pregnancy induced hypertension after receiving the structured teaching programme.

Table 17.3: comparison of mean and standard deviation of the pre and Post teaching knowledge scores regarding management of self among primigravida mothers with pregnancy induced hypertension

N=60

Sl. No.	*Knowledge on*	*Pre teaching*		*Post teaching*		*"t" value*
		Mean	*Standard deviation*	*Mean*	*Standard deviation*	
1	General information about pregnancy induced hypertension	23.45	6.21	82.30	10.56	29.93*
2	Management of self with pregnancy induced hypertension	26.07	6.56	83.00	13.00	29.77*
	Overall knowledge	24.61	4.75	72.67	14.55	5.410*

P< 0.05

Table 17.4 reveals that there was a significant increase in the overall knowledge regarding management of self with pregnancy induced hypertension among primigravida women after the structured teaching programme at ($P < 0.05$) level.

Association of selected demographic variables with the post teaching knowledge scores regarding management of self among primigravida mothers with pregnancy induced hypertension revealed that there was no significant association.

Discussion

The first objective of the study was to assess the existing knowledge regarding management of self among primigravida mothers with pregnancy induced hypertension and receiving care

The findings of the pre teaching knowledge scores revealed that among 60 samples majority 100% of the mothers had inadequate knowledge regarding management of self with pregnancy induced hypertension.

Since the primigravida mothers were new for pregnancy, they showed inadequate knowledge. This revealed that structured teaching programme is necessary for the primigravida mothers to improve their knowledge in the above aspects so that they can identify the warning signs on their own and can seek medical aid immediately which in turn contributes to the management of pregnancy induced hypertension.

The second objective of the study was to assess the knowledge regarding management of self among primigravida mothers with pregnancy induced hypertension and receiving care, after the structured teaching programme.

The findings of the post teaching knowledge scores revealed that among 60 samples majority 78% of the mothers had adequate knowledge regarding management of self with pregnancy induced hypertension.

These findings support the recommendations of **Pender (2000)** who identified that a known gap in the method of prevention and utilization of health care requires a dynamic type of education to help the women to understand the methods and engage in preventive health habits. He suggests that teaching on dietary habits, exercises, rest and health check up is important in the primary prevention and early detection of complications among high risk mothers.

The third objective of the study was to compare the pre and post teaching knowledge scores regarding management of self among primigravida mothers with pregnancy induced hypertension and receiving care.

The findings of the study revealed that there was a significant increase in the overall knowledge regarding management of self with pregnancy induced hypertension among primigravida women after the structured teaching programme at ($P < 0.05$) level.

This was supported by **Mullet et al (2004)** who suggested that structured teaching programme by the nurses is the valid mode of success for prenatal care.

The fourth objective of the study was to associate the knowledge scores regarding management of self among primigravida mothers with pregnancy induced hypertension and receiving care with selected variables.

The findings showed that statistically there was no significant association between the selected demographic variables with the post teaching knowledge scores regarding management of self among primigravida mothers with pregnancy induced hypertension.

Summary

The study findings were found to be in favor of the

researcher's assumption that the structured teaching programme will be an effective intervention for the primigravida mothers regarding management of self with pregnancy induced hypertension.

Conclusion

It was concluded that the structured teaching programme was effective in improving the knowledge of primigravida mothers regarding management of self with pregnancy induced hypertension.

Implications for Nursing

Nursing practice

- The midwives working in the antenatal unit must provide health education to the mothers with pregnancy induced hypertension regarding self care.
- Arrangements for the conduction of health awareness camps must be made in the hospitals and community areas for the antenatal mothers.

Nursing Education

- o Curriculum must be designed to provide opportunity for the student nurses to handle the high risk mothers.
- o Short term courses, in service education must be provided regularly to the staff nurses working in the obstetrical units.

Nursing Administration

- o Standard policy, protocols and standing orders must be developed to handle the antenatal mothers with pregnancy induced hypertension.
- o Conferences, seminars and training must be conducted to the staff nurses and the students

Recommendations

- The same study can be conducted in different settings.
- The study can also be conducted to assess the attitude and practice of the primigravida women regarding prevention of pregnancy induced hypertension.
- A longitudinal study can be done.
- A comparative study between the urban and rural population of primigravida mothers can also be conducted.

Suggestions

- To create awareness and knowledge, mass media should take active participation.
- Voluntary health agencies should indulge themselves in promoting health awareness.
- Adequate staff nurses have to be appointed in the health care settings by the government to provide quality and cost effective care.

References

- **Bobak and Jensen (2017)**. *Maternal Nursing.* Philadelphia: W.B. Saunders Company.
- **'Brien. P. (2008).** *Cost effective model for PIH.* Retrieved from www.pubmed.com
- **Pilliterrri, Adele (2016.)** *Maternal & Child Health Nursing* . Philadelphia: J.B. Lippincott Company.
- **Peggy (2000).** Health education in self care for hypertension. *Maternal & child Nursing* 24(5), 88-89.
- **Red man & Barbara Kelly (2000).** *The process of patient teaching in nursing.* St.Louis OV: Mosby Publications.
- **Saleh M & Selinger. M (2005).** *PIH and referral today assessment unit.* Retrieved from www.pubmed.com
- **Shear (2000)**. Hypertension in pregnancy & barriers to prenatal care in multiethnic urban sample. *Journal of Nurse Midwifery,* 30(2). 111-112.

- **Shanthakumari (1998)**. Planned health education on safe motherhood. *The Nursing Journal of India,* 37(10), 2226.
- **Walker J.J (2001).** Severe preeclampsia – best practice & research in clinical. Journal of Obstetrics & Gynecology, 14(1). 57–71.

Index

N

O

P